Alessandra Micalizzi
Editor

Computational Arts and Creative Products

Languages, Spaces and Practices

Copyright © 2025 by Nova Science Publishers, Inc.
DOI: https://doi.org/10.52305/GOFF2836

All rights reserved. No part of this book may be reproduced, stored in a retrieval system or transmitted in any form or by any means: electronic, electrostatic, magnetic, tape, mechanical photocopying, recording or otherwise without the written permission of the Publisher.

We have partnered with Copyright Clearance Center to make it easy for you to obtain permissions to reuse content from this publication. Simply navigate to this publication's page on Nova's website and locate the "Get Permission" button below the title description. This button is linked directly to the title's permission page on copyright.com. Alternatively, you can visit copyright.com and search by title, ISBN, or ISSN.

For further questions about using the service on copyright.com, please contact:
Copyright Clearance Center
Phone: +1-(978) 750-8400   Fax: +1-(978) 750-4470   E-mail: info@copyright.com

NOTICE TO THE READER

The Publisher has taken reasonable care in the preparation of this book, but makes no expressed or implied warranty of any kind and assumes no responsibility for any errors or omissions. No liability is assumed for incidental or consequential damages in connection with or arising out of information contained in this book. The Publisher shall not be liable for any special, consequential, or exemplary damages resulting, in whole or in part, from the readers' use of, or reliance upon, this material. Any parts of this book based on government reports are so indicated and copyright is claimed for those parts to the extent applicable to compilations of such works.

Independent verification should be sought for any data, advice or recommendations contained in this book. In addition, no responsibility is assumed by the Publisher for any injury and/or damage to persons or property arising from any methods, products, instructions, ideas or otherwise contained in this publication.

The Publisher assumes no responsibility for any statements of fact or opinion expressed in the published contents.

This publication is designed to provide accurate and authoritative information with regard to the subject matter covered herein. It is sold with the clear understanding that the Publisher is not engaged in rendering legal or any other professional services. If legal or any other expert assistance is required, the services of a competent person should be sought. FROM A DECLARATION OF PARTICIPANTS JOINTLY ADOPTED BY A COMMITTEE OF THE AMERICAN BAR ASSOCIATION AND A COMMITTEE OF PUBLISHERS.

Additional color graphics may be available in the e-book version of this book.

Library of Congress Cataloging-in-Publication Data

ISBN: 979-8-89530-426-6 (Softcover)
ISBN: 979-8-89530-499-0 (eBook)

Published by Nova Science Publishers, Inc. † New York

Contents

Foreword	The Challenges of Artificial Creativity .... v Francesco D'Isa	
Acknowledgments xi		
Chapter 1	Creating the "New" and the "Different": The Main Points of AI Applied to Creative Industries .... 1 Alessandra Micalizzi	
Chapter 2	The Role of Interactive Technology and Artificial Intelligence in Music Performance Practice and Research .... 13 Giusy Caruso	
Chapter 3	Synthesis: Interactive Intelligence .... 25 Mario Spada and Fabrizio Festa	
Chapter 4	Something Like Orpheus: Using AI to Make New Music to Hear the Past .... 47 Alessandro Ratoci and Clemence Martel	
Chapter 5	I-Artist: New Ways to Compose .... 67 Alessandro Camatta and Luca Ferliga	
Chapter 6	Doomed to Fantasize? Exploring the Implications of Critical Posthumanism for Creative Practices .... 83 Elisa Poli	
Chapter 7	Towards New Forms of Visual Narrative: AIneid, Virgil's Aeneid in the Age of AI .... 105 Fabio Morotti	

Chapter 8	**Conversational Artificial Intelligence and Autobiographical Writing**..............................125	
	Lara Balleri and Francesco Epifani	
Chapter 9	**The Impact of Artificial Intelligence on Creative Teaching: An Investigation of Education in the Technological Age**..137	
	Sabrina Lucilla Barone	

About the Editor 153

Contributors 155

Index 159

Foreword

The Challenges of Artificial Creativity

Francesco D'Isa[*]
Laba - Accademia di Belle Arti di Brescia, Italy

The topic of artificial creativity, as aptly named in this series of talks, is undeniably urgent. It's not just relevant for artists and creatives experimenting with these new tools, but also for situating this practice in a context where opinions are deeply divided. On one side, we have curious innovators; on the other, more conservative voices defending "traditional" art against new technologies—often forgetting that every traditional technique was, at one time, a disruptive innovation.

Despite the valid criticisms of these tools, it's hard not to notice parallels with past technological developments, such as the arrival of computer graphics, the internet, or photography, and even older inventions like the printing press or writing itself. In many cases, the critiques are strikingly similar—for instance, the claim that the printing press would destroy scribes' jobs or spread false information. But perhaps the most obvious analogy is with the birth of photography, which sparked a kind of revolt among traditional artists. In 1862, figures like Jean-Auguste-Dominique Ingres signed petitions such as the "Protest of Great Artists Against the Assimilation of Photography with Art," (Newhall, 1982) expressing concerns over photography's rapid development and its growing acceptance as an art form. Not all great artists joined this protest—Eugène Delacroix, for example, abstained—but notable figures like Honoré Daumier and Charles Baudelaire did. Baudelaire feared the ease of photography would lead to an explosion of mediocre works—and with hindsight, one might argue he was correct. His mistake, however, was in believing that photography could never produce true art. He was wrong, simply because he wasn't a photographer. We even have critiques from that era that echo today's arguments, like this quote from Lamartine, French Minister of Foreign Affairs, in 1848:

---

[*] Corresponding Author's Email: francesco.disa@gmail.com

"It is because of the servile nature of photography that I deeply despise this invention. It will never be art, but merely an optical copy of nature. Can a reflection of glass on paper be considered art? No, it's only a ray of sunlight caught by a machine. Where is the human intention? Where is the creative choice? Perhaps in the crystal, but certainly not in the man. The photographer can never replace the painter; one is human, the other is a machine. Let's stop comparing them." (p. 109, Tagg, 1993)

Replace "optical copy of nature" with "copy of artists' images in a dataset," and you have the standard critique of AI today. There's even the familiar complaint about the lack of "creative choice," a frequent objection whenever new automation emerges. These critiques of technologies we've since grown accustomed to may make us smile now, but they often contain a grain of truth. It's true the printing press and the internet have spread misinformation, just as photography flooded the world with low-quality images. Plato was right, too, when he said that writing would produce forgetfulness in the minds of those who relied on written records instead of memory. Or, as he wrote in Phaedrus, that writing would make us believe in things we have no direct knowledge of (Nehamas, Woodruff, 1995). In fact, no technology has spread more misinformation than writing itself—a phenomenon against which AI pales in comparison. But once our lives become shaped by these inventions, we can no longer muster the same passion for criticizing them as we do for attacking new tools. We've become accustomed to them, they've become part of us, and we know they've brought real benefits along with challenges.

That said, it's important to recognize that most generative AI tools are provided by private companies that charge high prices for proprietary software—software built using what I consider a public resource: data freely available on the internet. Rather than stigmatizing the creative use of these new tools or calling for their removal, the critique should shift towards advocating for open-source software—tools that are transparent, modifiable, and accessible to the public.

Despite the controversies, it's worth exploring cutting-edge work by artists who, with the genuine curiosity that defines creative minds, are experimenting—one might even say playing, in the noblest sense—with these tools. For example, in the project Synthesis (Spada, Festa), generative AI tools like ChatGPT, DALL-E, and AIVA show how art can evolve into an interactive experience where the audience shapes the visual and sound environment in real time. The concept of "collective intelligence" comes to life, with participants guiding the narrative and altering scenes based on their decisions.

Another compelling example is the I-Artist project (Camatta, Ferliga), where AI is integrated into every phase of the music creation process—from composition to post-production. Here, AI suggests melodies and harmonies, opening new creative possibilities without replacing the human touch, but enhancing it. This shows that while AI plays a significant role in the artistic process, the human element remains essential in refining and perfecting the final product.

In education, Sabrina Barone examines how AI is transforming creative teaching, showing how it can spark new methods that promote creativity among students and educators. Her work also addresses the ethical and practical challenges that arise with AI integration in education, showing that when used thoughtfully, these tools can enrich the learning experience.

Fabio Morotti, meanwhile, explores new forms of visual storytelling enabled by artificial intelligence. His research demonstrates how digital technologies are reshaping visual communication, blending creativity with tech to open fresh possibilities for storytelling.

Finally, in their study of creative autobiography, Lara Balleri and Francesco Epifani use AI to reflect on self-awareness through language, showing that AI can not only generate creative texts but also serve as a tool for analyzing those texts. In this context, AI acts as both co-author and analyst, offering a new perspective on narrative creation and interpretation.

AI-generated art forces us to rethink aesthetic experience. For those who value effort and human labor in art, what happens when the work is the product of a machine? This is an age-old dilemma. Consider Duchamp's Fountain, which starkly separated manual labor from artistic practice. There's little conceptual difference between a Renaissance artist delegating tasks to studio assistants and an artist today delegating tasks to a machine. Yes, human agency is involved, but we must also recognize the work of those using AI— work that can only be dismissed by those with little understanding of the medium. After all, Renaissance workshops relied on technologies of their time, like compasses, pantographs, camera obscuras, printing presses, and lathes. The use of machinery in art is not new; it has existed for centuries, and has only grown more powerful.

Though AI may mimic the role of the author, it is ultimately a tool—one that, like all technology (and more), has a degree of autonomy. No tool, not even the most "traditional" ones, is fully controlled by its user, and every technology has its own independence.

In painting, for example, the artist can only control their tools within the limits of the medium. They certainly can't dictate every interaction between the paint, the brush, and the canvas. Even though the painter chooses their own colors, these choices, besides being influenced by the work of other artists and visual trends, must comply with technical, economic, and production-related factors. Similarly, photographers rely heavily on their cameras, which interpret light and shadow in ways that can slip beyond their control. The same is true for sculptors: the interaction between chisel and stone can lead to unexpected outcomes, shaped by the material's structure and resistance. Each strike might reveal a hidden vein or cause an unforeseen crack, adding an element of chance to the creative process. Even in writing, the author never has full control; their words are shaped by the culture of the time, past readings, and linguistic conventions. Language speaks through us more than we speak through it, and while individual contributions can be significant, they are always influenced by the broader linguistic and cultural systems in which we operate. As I type on my keyboard, am I not essentially outsourcing my handwriting to a machine?

So, entrusting part of the creative process to technologies with some automation is nothing new. Avant-garde artists haven't been particularly shaken by AI's introduction into their work. Once we set aside anthropomorphic illusions and look at the work of creatives using these technologies, we find a long chain of human decisions and actions. However, the current climate doesn't foster open-minded exploration. Some artists face blacklists, canceled events, and misleading headlines in industry publications catering to anti-AI groups. The loudest opposition tends to come from comic artists and illustrators, both amateur and professional. Though they don't represent the entire creative community, their group is large and vocal.

Still, it would be shortsighted to dismiss many of the concerns being raised, since these tools are not without ethical issues, such as the indiscriminate collection of data to create software for private profit. This is problematic even for those of us (myself included) who believe that copyright has lost its effectiveness in protecting creators and spreading knowledge. From a public, collectivist perspective on data and AI, it's impossible to ignore the fact that very few companies release software as open source, meaning freely available and modifiable by anyone. The current battle, however, isn't focused on making AI public and accessible but rather on the conflict between the interests of big copyright holders and tech giants.

Despite the legitimacy of differing opinions, it's disheartening to see self-described creatives attacking anyone who tries to experiment with these new tools. "AI sucks, it'll never become part of the creative process!" they say, but if someone uses it (or is suspected of using it), they're immediately branded as a traitor. It's common to disguise conservatism with the phrase, "I'm not a Luddite, but"—and the "but" here is that artificial intelligence should neither be too powerful nor accessible to everyone: "Build your own datasets, pay for them!" This way, experimentation remains harmless, reserved only for the wealthy elite.

Meanwhile, many creatives are adopting these tools, albeit quietly and cautiously, because if you admit to using them, you're a sellout, and if you keep it secret, you're a coward. This phase inevitably mirrors the reception of photography, and the predictable outcome is a future where, once the excessive hype and fear have died down, these tools will be adopted by the majority, likely including those who criticize them today. If we were to conduct a casual survey, it seems that the strongest resistance to AI comes from those in the "applied arts." Designers and illustrators tend to be far more resistant than gallery artists, who have mostly embraced AI with curiosity. If this observation holds true, one reason could be that AI doesn't pose a threat to art itself, which has long digested the absence of manual labor and the delegation to automation. Instead, AI challenges digital craftsmanship, where the final product is consumed on a screen or in print, pre-processed digitally. It's almost as if digital craftsmanship stands in relation to AI the way landscape painters once did to photography—because photography has already eliminated the need for manual labor. That doesn't mean manual skill is losing its value. On the contrary, there will be areas, like non-digital craftsmanship, where it may become more valuable due to AI's existence. However, it is no longer essential. If I want to create an effective image, I no longer need to master manual techniques or even have access to complex equipment. It's no surprise, then, that many people who once relied on these skills now feel their vantage threatened. Not everyone, though—some have realized that their previous skills allow them to use AI more effectively in a hybrid approach, viewing it as an enhancement rather than a threat. In my experience teaching these tools in academia, I've noticed that after a year of coursework, students are using these new techniques in their own way, with a stylistically recognizable approach often blended with traditional practices, much to the dismay of those who believe "the computer does it all."

Artificial intelligence has already entered the world of art, though mostly within fields tied to new technologies and digital media, and we're still at the beginning. The tools currently accessible to the public have their limitations, and only a few people can push past them. But if the future leans more towards open and open-source AI, there's a strong chance we'll see the emergence of truly fascinating works. When evaluating AI-generated art, we must also remember that even when limited to traditional tools, the majority of what is produced is of mediocre quality. AI-generated works will be no exception—because, after all, they are still created by humans.

References

D'Isa F. *La Rivoluzione Algoritmica delle Immagini: Intelligenza Artificiale e Creatività*. Sossella; 2024.

Newhall B. *The History of Photography: From 1839 to the Present*. The Museum of Modern Art; 1982.

Tagg J. *The Burden of Representation: Essays on Photographies and Histories*. University of Minnesota Press; 1993.

Plato. Phaedrus. Nehamas A, Woodruff P, translators. Hackett Publishing Company; 1995.

Acknowledgments

This book is the result of a collective effort that began in October 2023. Its concrete realisation today is thanks to a working group of colleagues from Pegaso University, the Digital Humanities Research Centre, and the SAE Institute Academy in Milan. In particular, I would like to express my gratitude to Lara Balleri and Sara Selmi for their invaluable support in finalizing this work.

My sincere thanks also go to the publisher who believed in this project without hesitation.

I also owe a special thanks to the authors who, beyond their commitment to writing the chapters, dedicated time and effort to the editing process and responded patiently to my numerous requests.

I am also deeply grateful to my colleagues from P+Arts, the project that pushed me and my team to reflect on the impact of new technologies on applied arts and their roles in education.

The project is promoted and funded by the Ministry of University and Research and is part of a broader initiative funded by the European Union - Next Generation EU, Mission 4 component 1 CUP G43C24000640006.

Lastly, a heartfelt thanks to all of you who have chosen to read this book. Please share your thoughts with us, open spaces for discussion, and help us refine our research questions. On behalf of the entire board and the authors, I sincerely hope you find this work insightful and useful.

Chapter 1

Creating the "New" and the "Different": The Main Points of AI Applied to Creative Industries

Alessandra Micalizzi*, PhD
Department of Wellness, Nutrition and Sport, Pegaso University, Naples– SAE Institute, Milan, Italy

Abstract

This paper explores the intersection of artificial intelligence (AI) and creative production, focusing on how AI technologies influence the social construction of creativity, authorship, and artistic reproduction. The rapid integration of artificial intelligence into various domains has led to significant transformations, especially in the realm of creative practices. No longer limited to assisting humans in predefined tasks, AI now generates novel content across multiple media, from music and literature to visual art. This development necessitates a reassessment of creativity, authorship, and artistic value. AI's ability to autonomously produce creative works raises questions about originality and human involvement, mirroring earlier concerns about mechanical reproduction during the rise of photography and film. In this chapter, we explore these issues following the path already tracked by other scholars and offering an original contribution, presenting synthetically an interpretative model of users' perceptions about the use of AI in creative production.

Keywords: artificial creativity, deep learning, applied arts, generative AI, computational creativity, pop art, cultural products

---

* Corresponding Author's Email: alessandra.micalizzi@unipegaso.it; a.micalizzi@sae.edu

In: Computational Arts and Creative Products
Editor: Alessandra Micalizzi
ISBN: 979-8-89530-426-6
© 2025 Nova Science Publishers, Inc.

Arts and Creativity in the New Millennium

It is difficult to find a singular definition of creativity, as many disciplines have explored it, each emphasising a different perspective. Among human cognitive abilities, creativity has always sparked interest and curiosity due to its unique nature: for many, creativity is considered a distinctive trait of our species.

Is it a cognitive process? Does it coincide with the output? Is it a real human characteristic?

We cannot provide a definitive answer, but what we propose in the following pages is a selection of those perspectives that view creativity not merely as a psychological phenomenon internal to the individual but rather as a social practice that engages with other individuals, languages, cultures, and communicative processes.

We start with Rhodes (1961), who considers creativity "a phenomenon in which a person communicates a new concept." Rhodes developed the 4P model, which identifies four key elements that define a product as creative: the *product* itself, the *process* of its creation, the characteristics of the creator (the *person*), and the *place* or context, which is the result of the relationship between humans and their environment. This model highlights the importance of community recognition in determining whether something is considered creative. The environment also encompasses various factors—such as physical surroundings, social conditions, and personal wellbeing—that can indirectly influence the creative outcome. Simonton (2009) expanded upon this model by adding a fifth element, "persuasion," suggesting that art can function as a form of leadership.

Boden (1998) offers an interesting perspective on creativity, identifying the main elements that characterise a creative product: novelty, surprise, and value. In our attempt to offer a socio-cultural view on creativity, we find Boden's contribution extremely interesting, because he stressed the importance of the "value" that must be recognised by others. Moreover, he distinguishes between two types of novelty: psychological creativity, which is new to the individual creator, and historical creativity, which is new to society at large. This latter form aligns with what Kaufman and Beghetto (2009) term "Pro-C" creativity, which occurs within established domains and does not fundamentally challenge the paradigm.

In addition to Pro-C, we have everyday creativity, as discussed by Gruner and Csikszentmihalyi (2013). Sometimes referred to as "little-c creativity," it encompasses individuals' abilities to approach tasks in novel ways. Little-c creativity is largely shaped by emotional input, affective co-regulation, and human agency (Baker et al., 2017).

Scholars tend to differentiate between creativity used for small tasks and creativity destined to change the world, to be recognised as valuable, not only in a moral sense but also in an economic one. Moreover, they stress the importance of novelty: creativity offers new solutions, new ways to see the same things. For this reason, it is associated with discovery.

Csikszentmhalyi (1997:2014) contributes to a systemic vision of creativity. The proposed model includes three interrelated elements: an established and consensually accepted domain of current knowledge, an individual who modifies an aspect of that domain to generate something novel, and a field of experts who ultimately determine whether the novelty will be incorporated into the existing domain.

Thus, in the sociocultural approach, the individual is not the only determinant of the creative process, and creativity does not exist independently within any of these three elements. The community and the experts in the field and domain are crucial, as they must recognise creative production. In this model, the question shifts from "What is the creativity?" to "Where is it?" (Celis Bueno et al., 2024). This conceptual movement is extremely useful for the reflection about the integration of technologies in the coming pages.

Furthermore, the concept of creativity and its output is linked in some way to the concept of art, even if the two do not overlap. If we want to match creativity (particularly Pro-C) and art, we can simply recognise the touch points between the two words, which are represented in a particular way by products and output.

A quick framework of the concept of art can help to maintain the *fil rouge* of our discussion. Merriam-Webster (2024) defines art as "the conscious use of skill and creative imagination, especially in the production of aesthetic objects." This aligns with the positions of scholars who consider art the result of human intent, inspiration, and a desire to express something; for others, it is considered a purely cognitive activity. From these perspectives, art is the accomplishment of a specific task.

From a socio-cultural perspective, it seems that artistic expression loses its instinctual roots and is far from a response to the author's needs or urgency to communicate something. Duchamp (1957) argues that art is determined by the artist's intention, the institutional presentation, and the audience's reception, all of which serve as crucial steps in defining what constitutes art.

Similarly, Dickie (1974) maintains that the definition of art is contingent on the recognition and approval of the art world.

A human-centered definition of art is proposed by Hertsmann (2018), who states that art is fundamentally a social behavior. From this perspective, art is understood as "an interaction between social agents" emphasising the human element of artistic creation. This definition suggests that technical skill is not a prerequisite for someone to be considered an artist.

Using the philosophy of Wittgeinstein, we can say that something is art if it is recognised by specific and subjective processes:

> We rely on a self-reflective consciousness of social context, resemblances, and associations in order to recognize something as belonging to a perceptual category such as art. (…) so it follows, that an image generated by AI has the abstracted properties and resemblances needed to identify it with perceptual class, then it becomes a member of that class. (Smith & Cook, 2023, p. 2)

To summarise, art production and creativity are not the same thing, but they move in the same scenario, where personal intentions find expression in outputs that require socio-cultural validation.

The Computational Process Toward "Newness": A Framework

In this scenario, we can collocate the debate about the connection between arts (and creativity) and technologies. Without going into depth, it is important for the purpose of this paper to stress that artistic languages, techniques, and products have been always contaminated by technologies: cameras, for example, have intervened inexorably in the reproducibility of artistic images (Benjamin, 1963). Scholars do not often highlight the parallelism between the advent of photography and the application of AI in creative production (Kalpokas, 2023).

Generative AI can learn to be more autonomous in production and make certain decisions. More specifically, while GANs (generative adversarial networks) are limited to replicating a specific creative style, CANs (creative adversarial networks) can diverge from the learned style, enabling the generation of novel and potentially creative works (Liu, 2023).

Thanks to the widespread use of AI tools in the production of texts, images, and other cultural products, discussions surrounding creativity and the "artistic value" of AI-generated content have become strikingly urgent. At the same time, the rise of these technologies raises questions about the influence of technology on the concept, status, and role of art, as well as the position of these new methods of (re)producing reality within that framework and the relation to the construction of our imagery (Kalpocas, 2023).

Does the intersection of human creativity and AI produce new forms of art? Can we define "creativity" differently than we did in the past? How can we define it?

The notion of computational creativity (Colton & Wiggins, 2012) or artificial creativity is increasingly relevant in scientific debate. This expression refers to the application of artificial intelligence to generate novel and valuable creative outputs through the systematic extraction and processing of structured and unstructured forms of data (Eshraghian, 2020).

Artificial intelligence (AI) has emerged as a crucial tool within creative industries, by optimising production processes that require specific thinking tasks (Anantrasirichai & Bull, 2022). The impact of AI leads to the facilitation of processes, the reduction of costs, and the scalability of production in a field (creativity) that has always required time.

Over the past decade, AI has acquired capabilities to "see," "hear," "speak," "move," and "write," and has thus been applied across a wide range of fields and applications, including audio, image and video analysis, gaming, journalism, screenwriting, filmmaking, and social media analysis (Machado et al., 2021).

To cite some examples: GANs (generative adversarial networks) have been employed in visual art, as in the transformation of portrait images into dynamic video representations. The use of AI for artistic creation extends beyond tangible outputs like paintings and fashion products to intangible creations like music (Cope, 2005; Li et al., 2010). Given the economies of scale and novel experiences that AI enables in the arts, a range of consumer-oriented solutions for music composition and production have emerged in recent years.

Zeilinger (2021) argues that AI "has the potential to reshape the aesthetic, cultural, and socio-economic dimensions of creativity," thereby destabilising the traditional notion of the author. AI-generated art, he notes, is "fundamentally based on Big Data, which is the most social thing we have." This challenges the Western conception of human primacy and instead promotes an understanding of life as "an ongoing composition in which humans and non-humans participate." In this view, everyday realities take on a "more-than-human" character, with assemblages and interconnections between human, digital (data, algorithms, AI), and physical elements (Zeilinger, 2021).

From this perspective, we can consider Esposito's (2017) view that, in a wider sense not strictly connected to art production, defines AI as an artificial communication, trying to overcome the direct comparison to human abilities and abandoning the idea of something that is "intelligent." From Esposito's perspective, AI is dialogical, interpersonal, and based on interaction.

AI-generated art is never entirely machine-driven or detached from human experience; rather, it is intricately linked to human expression and perceptions of the world. Since AI creativity is built upon data, its core function is to reorganise information in ways that are both novel and recognisable to human audiences. While this execution of creativity is machinic, it does not emerge from any specific machine aesthetics or sensitivities. As a result, the aesthetics of AI-generated art remain, at least for now, centered on human sensibilities in terms of both the learning process and the intended audience.

We want to stress that, in the public debate, there is less space for critical and skeptical positions on the use of AI in tasks that are considered human prerogatives. An integration of human intentions and technological practices will define a new scenario where data, human beings, and AI can collaborate. Indeed, the incorporation of AI highlights a distinctly posthuman dimension by introducing a new – artificial – form of agency into the reciprocal interactions between humans and data, transforming them into a triangular relationship involving humans, data, and AI.

On the one hand, we have scholars who state that "the notion that a machine learning system could produce art or be regarded as an artist is implausible, as an artist cannot be reduced to a mere machine with intent." On the other hand, we can extend Duchamp's concept of art to AI-generated products to the extent that the action operated by machine learning is a process of selection (ivi, 1957). We espouse Hertzman's (2018) vision of art as a form of interaction, in which AI tools are just a medium -- a part of the process, a co-protagonist of new ways of creating that will be defined by artists, technologies, and societies. Finally, we agree with Navas (2023), who introduces the concept of "meta-creativity," defined as "a cultural variable that emerges when the creative process goes beyond human production to include non-human systems" (Hertzman, 2018, as cited in D'Isa, 2024, p. 137). Our recent research on the impact of AI-generative creative production on the public's perception revealed the need to identify a neat distinction between what is art and what is simply an output of a cultural process (Micalizzi, 2024).

Our respondents proposed a new label, *augmented creativity*, to identify these shared skills and tasks among humans and technologies. This can offer an interesting view on the topic and its future developments.

Creative Practices and Experience: A New Vision of Applied Art

We will now take a step back to Csikszentmhalyi. With the introduction of AI, he proposed a new version of his model, to describe the so-called "Creativity 4.0."

The model introduces AI and connects it with individuals and domains. With the integration of AI, individuals or groups develop rule-based algorithms that enable computational modeling, pattern recognition, and predictive capabilities. Rather than receiving direct inputs from the environment, the AI is programmed to adapt to the information it encounters within the domain, thereby expanding and modifying the potential for new permutations (Atkinson & Barker 2023).

However, if we recall the definition of art and creativity proposed in the first section, we can see that this model underestimates the role of society -- that is the importance of being recognized, culturally and socially, as a product of art.

Several studies (among others Latikka et al., 2023) highlight how users are unprepared to identify what is produced by AI, even if some forms of bias remain. At the beginning of the discussion about artificial creativity, respondents pointed out the low quality of AI-generated productions, but blind tests found this to be based more on prejudice than on real evidence (Micalizzi, 2024). In recent years, awareness has increased, and the public is increasingly open to appreciating the quality of AI's creative outputs and accepting the difficulties of distinguishing what was created by AI and what was not. Several studies have demonstrated a growing acceptance of artificially created or co-created products (Hong, 2021). For instance, research (Elgammal et al., 2017) shows that AI can be employed to produce automated artworks that consumers cannot distinguish from human-created ones. Elgammal and colleagues (2017) further discovered that machine-generated products were often preferred over human-made ones, receiving higher scores on attributes such as novelty, complexity, intentionality, and inspiration. Similarly, Hadjeres et al., (2017) used a generative model called DeepBach to create new compositions based on the works of Johann Sebastian Bach. In tests, nearly half of participants categorised the AI-generated music as "original." However, the results indicated that as musical expertise increased, fewer participants (40%) believed the machine-generated music was composed by Bach.

These findings were later corroborated by experimental studies, including those by Hong and Curran (2019) and Tigre Moura et al., (2021), which revealed that while respondents held somewhat negative views of AI music composition, knowing that AI was involved had minimal impact on their perception of the resulting compositions.

We would like to stress that in the process of recognising AI-generated products as a form of creativity and artistic expression, some variables intervene: the level of awareness about or the opacity of the use of these technologies in art production; the biases connected with the old-fashioned perception of AI as rational, unemotional, and unable to reproduce typical human skills (confirmed by several experiments); and the weight of the ethical issues connected to authorship and the value of the artistic production.

Each point raised above represents a crucial point in the public debate about the complex topic of art, AI, and socio-cultural implications. In these pages, we aim to offer an interpretation of the phenomenon that, in some ways, disconnects the concept of art from the product in the strict sense, and from a dialogical and cultural perspective, stresses the role of the experience.

If we emphasise the experience as the pivotal moment of "having art," art can be considered a verb, as suggested by Ketie Compton (2022). The author abandons the old categories for defining an artwork– the author, the materiality, the cultural value, etc. – to instead focus on the experience, recontextualising the concept of art within Bauman's metaphor of post-modernity. In this way, art also becomes liquid, in contrast to the "solid" and monolithic view of the past.

Liquid art (ivi) can be defined as a space of potential artistic artifacts, navigated through the act of surfing and filtering and experienced as streams or overwhelming waves, most commonly in an online environment. It refers to the phenomenon of encountering mass-produced artifacts, such as AI-generated imagery, in a context where their sheer abundance transforms the act of "surfing" through this media into the experience of art itself (Smith & Cook 2023). The centrality of experience in creating (liquid) art redefines the role of AI, which becomes one of the elements at play in the dialogical process between artist, society, culture, and artifact.

Even from this perspective, the ethical question regarding the use of sources and referentiality, as well as the impact on public imagination and tastes, remains open. This is particularly relevant in relation to a quantitatively infinite production that is still limited in variety and primarily focused on generating approval (audience interest) rather than innovating or conveying a message (author's intentions). We can only hope for a more open and trusting attitude that can lead towards experimentation, while adhering to ethically sound objectives.

Maybe it is possible to imagine a new way to observe and frame art and creativity in their relationship with technologies. It may be possible to overcome the topic of authorship if we use the perspective proposed by D'Isa (2024), the author who opens this publication. Provocatively, D'Isa asks an important question: what is the true innovation brought by AI in its connection with the art world? D'Isa argues that we should see the artwork as the result of multiple factors, in which we traditionally isolate the human as the author. He suggests that "the shock caused by innovation has momentarily disrupted an interpretive habit, reminding us that it is not we who create, but the world" (ivi, p. 145).

Disclaimer

This contribution is part of a project funded by Uuropean Union- Next Generation EU, Mission 4 component 1 CUP G43C24000640006.

References

Anantrasirichai, N., & Bull, D. Artificial intelligence in the creative industries: A review. *Artificial Intelligence Review*, 55 (2022): 1– 68.
Atkinson P., Barker R. AI and the social construction of creativity. *Convergence: the international journal of research into new media technologies.* 2023. 29(4): 1054-1069.
Baker, C. L., Jara-Ettinger, J., Saxe, R., & Tenenbaum, J. B. Rational quan- titative attribution of beliefs, desires and percepts in human mentalizing. Nature Human Behaviour, (2017): 1-4.
Boden M. Creativity and artificial intelligence. Artif Intell (1998) 103:347–356.
Benjamin, W. The Work of Art in the Age of Its Technological Reproducibility. In *Philosophers on Film from Bergson to Badiou: A Critical Reader*: (2019 ed 1963) 44-79. Columbia University.

Boreham, R., & Wijnant, A. Developing a web-smartphone-telephone questionnaire. In *IBUC 2013 15th International Blaise Users Conference*. *Washington* DC Available (2013) at: http://www.blaiseusers.org/2012/papers/04b.pdf.

Celis Bueno C., Choe P. S, Popowicz A., Not "what" but "where" is creativity?": towards a relational-materialist approach to generative AI. *AI & Society* (2024): 22/04.

Csikszentmihalyi, M. Creativity: *Flow and the psychology of discovery and invention.* (1996) New York: HarperCollins.

Csikszentmihalyi M. *Society, culture, and person: a systems view of creativity. The systems model of creativity.* (2014) Dordrecht: Springer: 47–61.

Colton, S., & Wiggins, G. A. Computational creativity: The final frontier?. In *ECAI 2012*: 21-26. IOS Press.

Compton, K. Ter- rible together: A creativity manifesto. http://aialchemy.media.mit.edu/terrible-together.html. (2022) [Accessed: 22/09/2024].

Cope, D. *Computer models of musical creativity* (2005) Cambridge, MA: MIT Press.

D'Isa F. *La rivoluzione algoritimica delle immagini. Arte e Intelligenza artificiale.* (2024) Rome: Luca Sossella Editore.

Dickie G. Art and the aesthetic: an institutional analysis. (1974) Cornell University Press, Ithaca, NY.

Duchamp, M. The creative act. *Art News (1957):*56(4).

Eshraghian, J. K. Human ownership of artificial creativity. *Nature Machine Intelligence*, (2020):2: 157–160.

Elgammal, A., Liu, B., Elhoseiny, M., & Mazzone, M. CAN: Creative Adversial Networks generating "art" by learning about styles and deviating from style norms. *arXiv preprint arXiv* (2017) :1706.07068.

Esposito E. "Artificial Communication? The Production of Contingency by Algorithms." *Zeitschrift für Soziologie* (2017) 46, (2): 249–265.

Gruner, D. T., & Csikszentmihalyi, M. Engineering creativity in an age of artificial intelligence. *The Palgrave handbook of social creativity research* (2019):47-462.

Hernandez-Olivan, C., Hernandez-Olivan, J., & Beltran, J. R. A survey on artificial intelligence for music generation: Agents, domains and perspectives. *arXiv preprint arXiv*: (2022)2210.13944.

Hertzmann A. Can computers create art? *Arts* (2018) 7(2):18.

Maleki, N., Padmanabhan, B., & Dutta, K. AI hallucinations: a misnomer worth clarifying. In *2024 IEEE Conference on Artificial Intelligence (CAI)* (2024): 133-138 IEEE.

Hadjeres, G., Pachet, F., & Nielsen, F. (2017). Deepbach: A steerable model for bach chorales generation. In *Proceedings of the 34th international conference on machine learning* 70 (2017). 1362–1371). Sydney, *Australia: International Conference on Machine Learning*.

Hong, JH. Artificial Intelligence (AI), Don't Surprise Me and Stay in Your Lane: An Experimental Testing of Perceiving Humanlike Performances of AI. *Human Behavior and Emerging Technologies* 3(5) 2021: 1023–32.

Hong, J. W., & Curran, N. M. Artificial intelligence, artists, and art: Attitudes toward artwork produced by humans vs. artificial intelligence. *ACM Transactions on Multimedia Computing, Communications, and Applications* (TOMM), (2019):15, 1–16.

Kaufman, J. C., & Beghetto, R. A. (2009). Beyond big and little: The four C model of creativity. *Review of General Psychology, 13* (2009):1–12.

Kalpokas, I. Work of art in the Age of Its AI Reproduction. *Philosophy & Social Criticism*, (June 2023).

Latikka R., Bergdhal J., Savela N. Oksanen A., AI as an artist? A two-wave survey study on attitudes toward using artificial intelligence. *Poetics* (2023): 101839.

Lee HK. Rethinking creativity: creative industries, AI and everyday creativity. *Media Cult Soc* (2022): 44(3):601–612.

Li, T. L., Chan, A. B., & Chun, A. H. Automatic musical pattern feature extraction using convolutional neural network. Genre, (2010): 10, 1x1.

Liu, B. Arguments for the Rise of Artificial Intelligence Art: Does AI Art Have Creativity, Motivation, Self-awareness and Emotion? *Arte, Individuo y Sociedad*, (2023): *35*(3), 811.

Machado, P., Romero, J., & Greenfield, G. *Artificial intelligence and the arts-computational creativity, artistic behavior, and tools for creatives.* (2021) Switzerland: Springer.

Malabau C. *Morphing intelligence: from IQ measurement to artificial brains.* (2019) NY: Columbia University Press.

Maleki, N., Padmanabhan, B., & Dutta, K. AI hallucinations: a misnomer worth clarifying. In *2024 IEEE Conference on Artificial Intelligence (CAI)* IEEE (2024): 133-138.

Manovich, L. (2020). *Cultural analytics*. Cambridge: Mit Press.

Manovich, L. (2018). *AI aesthetics*. Moscow: Strelka press.

Manovich L., Arielli E. *Artificial Aesthetics: A Critical Guide to AI, Media and Design*, available at https://manovich.net/content/04-projects/175-artificial-aesthetics/ artificial_aesthetics.chapter_1.pdf 2021: 4-27. [accessed 09/09/2024].

Manovich L. Arielli E. *Artificial Aesthetics: Generative AI, Art and Visual Media.* Available at https://manovich.net/index.php/projects/artificial-aesthetics (2024). [accessed 09/07/2024].

Micalizzi A. Artificial Creativity. Perceptions and Prejudices on AI Music Productions. In X. S. Yang et al. (eds.), *Proceedings of Ninth International Congress on Information and Communication Technology*, (2024) Lecture Notes in Networks and Systems 1004.

Merriam-Webster *Art*. Available at https://www.merriam-webster.com/dictionary/art [accessed 22/09/2024].

Micalizzi A. Lelicanin M. *Studiare i creative media. Ricerca e analisi dei processi di creazione, condivisione e appropriazione culturale.* (2023) Novara: Utet Università.

Navas E. *The rise of metacreativity. IA Aestetics after remix.* (2023) London-New York: Routledge.

Tigre Moura, F., Castrucci, C., & Hindley, C. Artificial intelligence creates art? An experimental investigation of value and creativity perceptions. *The Journal of Creative Behavior*, (2023): *57*(4): 534-549.

Rhodes, M. An analysis of creativity. *The Phi Delta Kappan*, (1961) 42:305–310.

Simonton, D. Varieties of (scientific) creativity: A hierarchical model of domain-specific disposition, development, and achievement. *Perspectives on Psychological Science, (2009) 4*: 441–452.

Smith, A., & Cook, M. AI-Generated Imagery: A New Era for theReadymade'. In *SIGGRAPH Asia 2023 Art Papers* (2023): 1-4.

Tigre Moura, F., Castrucci, C., & Hindley, C. Artificial intelligence creates art? An experimental investigation of value and creativity perceptions. *The Journal of Creative Behavior*, *57*(4), (2023): 534-549. Verbick, T. Women, technology, and gender bias. *Journal of Computing Sciences in Colleges*, (2002): *17*(3), 240-250.

Zeilinger, Martin. Generative Adversarial Copy Machines. *Culture Machine* 2021: 20: 1–23.

Chapter 2

The Role of Interactive Technology and Artificial Intelligence in Music Performance Practice and Research

Giusy Caruso[*], **PhD**
Department of Music, Royal Conservatoire Antwerp, Belgium

Abstract

This chapter presents an overview on the integration of interactive technology and generative AI in music performance practice and research. The state-of-the-art in creative applications and the impact of digital technologies on the current music scenario will be defined here by highlighting potentialities and challenges. While digital advancements have already transformed music communication and expression, further studies are needed to develop new creative methodologies and applications in music performance, composition, improvisation and digital instrument design. Multidisciplinary competence and exchange of knowledge drawn from art, science, and technology are recommended along with ethical considerations to ensure that technological advancements enhance, rather than diminish, the artistic value of music creation. Beyond these reflections, interactive technology and AI are inevitably moving music performance practice and research towards new techno-aesthetic paradigms.

Keywords: interactive technology, artificial intelligence, artistic research, music performance practice, embodied cognition

---

[*] Corresponding Author's Email: giusy.caruso@ap.be

In: Computational Arts and Creative Products
Editor: Alessandra Micalizzi
ISBN: 979-8-89530-426-6
© 2025 Nova Science Publishers, Inc.

Introduction

The development of interactive technology actively influences innovative trajectories for music creation and research (Lessaffre & Leman, 2020). Interactive technology refers to systems and devices designed for real-time applications, immediate feedback, and adaptation, enabling dynamic interplay between user and environment. It includes various gestural technologies, biosensors, motion tracking, and IoT —the Internet of Things, a network of interrelated devices that connect and exchange data. Nowadays, these technologies are also extended to immersive experiences of augmented reality (AR) and virtual reality (VR) implying the use of Artificial Intelligence (AI), which has evolved from purely experimental research fields into versatile toolsets applicable across various domains, including music creation.

Interactive technology and AI have challenged traditional modalities of production, consumption and diffusion of music (De Assis et al., 2024; Saunders et al., 2022). Artists, researchers, and performers are often spurred on using up-to-date technology to improve their expressivity or simply analyze their performance practice. . Interactive technology and AI have thus become pivotal tools to enhance traditional methods of creating and studying music.

The premises on collaborative and co-creative strategies in art, science, and technology set in this chapter draw an overview of the studies and application of specific interactive technologies. Some examples are motion tracking and wearable biosensor in music performance practice and generative AI models in music composition, improvisation and digital instrumental design. Such framework makes it possible to describe and reflect on state-of-the-art applications and impact of digital technologies on the current music scenario. Cutting-edge devices and tools that enhance creativity will be described and illustrated by focusing on their potential usages. . Challenges will necessarily emerge regarding competencies and skills required by this multidisciplinary approach to facilitate knowledge exchange between art, science, and technology (Caruso & Nijs, 2021). Since advancements in digital technologies have revolutionized the ways we communicate, express, and transmit music across different cultures and societies (Born, 2022),additional studies are expected on new methodologies and applications in music creation and research.

Motion Tracking Technology and Embodied Cognition in Research on Music Performance Practice

In the last decades, research on music has been focused on investigating body movements in performance, specifically the relationship between gesture and sound within the theoretical framework of embodied cognition (Leman, 2007). The theory of embodied cognition is grounded on the interaction between bodily movement and cognitive states; in simpler words, the mind is not only connected to the body, but also that the body influences the mind (Varela et al., 1991). In music performance, corporeal gestures are employed to realize musical goals as final sonic outcome when playing an instrument, for example. (Leman, 2007). To track performers' gestures and to define a vocabulary of movements that produces music on an instrument, computational methods and biofeedback technologies have been applied in diverse empirical studies. In particular, motion capture technology (MoCap) has been used to analyze gesture and physiological data of performers in relation to the interpretation and execution of a musical score (see Caruso, 2018; Caruso et al., 2016; Desmet et al., 2012; Wanderley et al., 2005). The data acquired during a motion recording consist of quantitative measurements of the body in performance according to the Cartesian coordinate system. Furthermore, the captured measurements of gestures can be turned into a digital 3D virtual agent of the performer (avatar). This technique offers a better visualization of the body posture and choreography of a performer compared to the 2D dimensions of traditional video recordings because the 3D virtual image can be rotated and seen from different viewpoints.

The application of motion capture recording, mainly used in systematic musicology, has been then extended - to artistic research in music under the paradigm of "technology-enhanced mirror" (Caruso et al. 2021; Caruso et al. 2016). This method was developed with the artistic purpose to assist musicians in the processes of documenting, analyzing and disseminating their music performance practice as a research work. Artistic research in music normally requires that performer-researchers explain and analyze their own creative process; they collect data on their own music performance to be assembled, evaluated and disseminated as new knowledge. Traditional ways of documenting and presenting music performance practice in a research work implied reflective methods (Schön, 1984) to collect verbal or written qualitative descriptions, such as diaries, reports, interviews, dialogues etc. (see Schwab & Borgdorff, 2014).

Documentation is gathered here from the performer's first-person perspective with the risk, however, of being subjective and deprived of important information in the process of embodiment on how the body moves and interacts with the performance space, the instrument, the musical score or other musicians during a music performance. Motion capture technology, on the other hand, quantitatively tracks gestural qualities. proving significant measurements of gesture. This is crucial information for artists and researchers involved in the observation, improvement and description of their own performance practice. Consequently, motion capture technology can be seen as an augmented 'mirroring' tool that can guide musicians and artist-researchers in monitoring and mapping movements in relation to interpretation and execution (Caruso et al., 2021).

The paradigm of "technology-enhanced-mirror" employs a mixed methodology that integrates empirical data with artistic insights. Thus, quantitative data on movements, embedded into artistic practice, can support performers' subjective reflections, descriptions and intuitions. On the one hand, technology can help musicians in the evaluation and observation of their performance practice because performers can analyze and evaluate their way of playing an instrument from a meta-perspective (Tam et al., 2023; Goebl et al., 2014); on the other hand, digital data give more accurate documentation on music performance which can be studied by researchers and shared as new knowledge. This approach will consequently contribute to bridging the gap between empirical studies and artistic practice by opening new frontiers, fostering innovative methods in research on music performance practice.

Augmented Reality (AR) and Virtual Reality (VR) in Immersive Music Experiences

Recently, the use of motion tracking in research on music has been extended to augmented and virtual reality (AR/VR). AR and VR enable researchers to simulate insights and observe phenomena as they would in the real world, without interference. Compared to conventional empirical research methods in laboratory context and real performance space, this approach presents contradictions and challenges. This is because it offers limited control over stimuli and often encounters difficulties with reliable measurements (for example, in the motion capture of a performance, there can be problems with marker occlusions due to interference from the infrared light). However, the alternative would be to continue with traditional empirical experiments conducted in conventional spaces, which often lack ecological validity, making it difficult to achieve generalizable results (Van Kerrebroeck et al., 2021). Considering the digital process involved in creating augmented and immersive contexts, AR and VR technology provide flexibility in data recording methods and options. This flexibility is particularly beneficial in the study of social music interaction, where establishing a social presence is key. The goal of these studies is to examine social interactions within immersive environments that facilitate multisensory engagement with virtual settings, digital entities, and individuals (Maes et al., 2024; Kyrlitsias & Michael-Grigoriou, 2022). The output of these studies has also led to the artistic creation of augmented performance where the physiological implications of performers are shown in real time as a performative element (Caruso 2019, Antoniadis et al., 2022).

Our current societal context, influenced by new perspectives on remote art consumption, inspired a reimagined spatial framework for performers and spectators and stimulated further explorations and reflections of the physicality and interactivity of bodies and avatars in virtual environments. These experimentations spurred empirical studies on the social presence and flow of the audience attending performances in virtual environments, especially during the pandemic (Onderdijk et al., 2023). The expansion of the interconnection from different locations brought new possibilities for performing in hybrid performance spaces, where real stages encounter virtual stages. This perspective provoked the creation of extended music performances in which musicians interact in virtual environments (Timmerman & Vanoeveren, 2024) and with their avatars in the metaverse (Caruso, 2024), thereby enhancing the audience's perception and engagement.

The term "metaverse" – originally taken from dystopian narratives in novels like *Snow Crash* (1992) by Neal Stephenson and *Ready Player One* (2011) by Ernest Cline – is described as a post-reality universe where physical reality and digital virtuality converge. In spite of the misuse of the term by social networks to indicate the interconnections of people represented as avatars on the internet, immersive experiences in the metaverse imply the convergence of technologies that enable multisensory interactions with virtual environments, digital objects, and people. Playing in a virtual world provides performers with a new perception and proprioception—which refers to one's ability to perceive the position, movement, and actions of different parts of their own body, as well as their interaction with the surrounding space (Stillman et al., 2002). Additionally, spectators' imagination is also challenged in terms of the objects perceived, as well as their sense of presence, flow, and time in relation to a performance.

In the context of music performance, studying social presence can significantly enhance the understanding of social music cognition and interaction in two main ways. It encourages to reflect on and broaden the definition of the essential elements of human social cognition and sense-making (Blascovich et al., 2002) and it allows for the precise manipulation and adjustment of the many factors that influence a musical interaction, including the context in which the interaction occurs. Although technological proficiency is required, research methods using AR and VR are becoming increasingly accessible and standardized, thereby offering representative sampling and improved replicability.

Developments will aim to make the performance space more immersive and interactive, allowing performers and avatars to interact from different locations, breaking down the boundaries of physical space and moving toward more immersive and extended experiences.

Artificial Intelligence (AI) and Machine Learning (ML) as Music Tools

AI and ML have transitioned from being purely experimental research areas to becoming versatile toolsets with a wide range of applications. While text generation (e.g., ChatGPT) and image generation (e.g., DALL-E) have seen significant breakthroughs and public adoption, tools for musical generation have not yet achieved the same level of widespread use and artistic integration. AI algorithms assist artists in various ways: neural networks, particularly deep learning algorithms, can learn, process, and replicate patterns and stylistic elements of musical material. Additionally, evolutionary computation enables the management of more complex musical systems without the need for explicitly defined generation methods.

Different studies and works have addressed interactive AI modeling in the fields of music composition, improvisation, and the design of digital musical instruments. ML provides the framework and methodologies to instruct a system to learn from and make decisions based on a certain dataset. This is the case of EMG signals, for example, that can instruct models from the electrical signals generated by muscle tensions electrically or neurologically activated. The evolution of wearable devices supported by machine learning (ML) has introduced novel interactive strategies for exploring the motion and physiological sensing of performers' bodies, which can directly generate music and visuals. Some studies are focused on Gestural Interface (GI) for gesture-controlled digital instruments and multi-sensory audiovisual generative systems. Interactions have been created by applying wearable biosensors to performers' muscles connected to software, such as Max/MSP-Cycling '74, for sound and visual programming language (Visi & Tanaka 2021, Zbyszynsk, et al., 2020; Rhodes et al., 2020; Tanaka et al., 2019; Tanaka and Donnarumma 2019). These sensors have embedded ML capabilities to track and process the gesture and muscle tensions of a performer. Biodata can then be labeled, organized and transformed into sound and visuals through Max/MSP software (see Kanga 2022; Caruso & Eldem 2022). Beside the studies on gestural interface, current research also includes the analysis and mapping of the electrophysiological signals of the brain to transform them into sound through flexible, modular and user-friendly interfaces (Tanaka et al., 2023; Di Maggio et al., 2023).

Some recent advancements in? audio modeling enabled new forms of interaction, such as unconditional generation in music composition and improvisation (Gioti et al. 2023 Dhariwal et al., 2020; Vasquez & Lewis, 2019) while some traced the transfer of timbre between instruments (Caillon & Esling 2021; Mor et al., 2018). Other research projects investigate human-machine co-improvisation by developing interactive and generative AI models (see Somax2 by Assayag et al., 2022; Fiorini et al., 2024).

Audio generative models, such as RAVE (*Realtime Audio Variational Autoencoder model,* Caillon & Esling, 2021), were explored by the research group CREATION at the Royal Conservatoire Antwerp (RCA) in the project AI-Musicking 2024 for music improvisation. Extensive audio recordings gathered from musicians during various recording sessions were used to create a dataset of samples that were examined, collected, and labeled in order to train the RAVE model (*Realtime Audio Variational Autoencoder model*). The resulting trained model was explored through co-creative sessions involving different researchers and musicians. The goal was to examine human-machine interactions in interactive music performances based on real-time improvisations with the system's responses.

Concerning digital musical instrument design, the IMAREV research project at IRCAM produced the 'Smart Instrument,' which has been commercialized by the HyVibe sound tech company. This instrument provides new possibilities for performance, composition, and education by incorporating features such as real-time sound synthesis, gesture recognition, and connectivity with other digital devices (Meurisse et al., 2014; Benacchio et al., 2012, 2016). While Calegario et al., (2017) developed Digital Musical Instruments (DMIs) based on action–sound mappings, where the physical energy of the input action does not necessarily correspond to the output sound. Other researchers introduced the use of smart instruments that allow users to retrieve songs from online music databases using unconventional search criteria, such as tempo, chords, key, and tuning, rather than metadata like song title or artist name (see the guitar prototype by Turchet et al., 2020).

This overview on the use of AI and ML into musical practice shows how generative models can enhance rather than hinder artistic expression. The aesthetic concerns of creative collaboration with machine learning tools for instrument building and performance provide practical insights into new forms of expressivity and control, which can contribute to developing relationship between musicians and instruments (Fiebrink and Sonami 2020).

Discussion and Conclusion

The progression of recent applications of interactive technology and artificial intelligence in music has significantly transformed artistic creation and research. These advancements have enabled artists to explore new dimensions of expression and interaction, pushing the boundaries of traditional music performance, composition, improvisation and digital instrument design. Motion capture technology allows for precise analysis and real-time feedback on performers' movements, enhancing both the technical and expressive aspects of music, and research. Meanwhile, AI algorithms offer innovative tools for generating, analyzing and manipulating musical content facilitating, at times, complex creative processes.

As these technologies continue to evolve, they promise to revolutionize the field, fostering a deeper understanding of the interplay between human creativity and technological innovation. This ongoing progression not only enriches the artistic scenario but also opens up new avenues for interdisciplinary research and collaboration, ultimately leading to a more dynamic and inclusive musical ecosystem. The framework of embodied music cognition and mediation technology, and the studies on human-machine interaction (HMI) and artificial intelligence provide the theoretical and technical ground for new artistic experimentations in music performance practice.

The intersection of art, science, and technology is a contemporary challenge that unlocks new possibilities in music performance analysis, research, and production. By drawing from these recent studies on embodied music cognition, mediation technology, and innovative performance strategies, it is evident that collaborative and co-creative approaches seem necessarily plausible. Despite the rapid technological advancement and close scrutiny of AI generation, the development of an artistic methodology and framework for contemporary musical human-machine in co-creative practices still remains a field to be largely explored. This area requires further investigations to understand the current and potential future impact of these tools on such practices. The primary issue lies in developing user-friendly methodologies that can enhance music performance practice, creation, and research. This challenge highlights the necessity for accessible applications and methods tailored for musicians. Even though technological expertise is required, research practices are becoming more standardized and accessible, leading to representative sampling and enhanced replicability. Artist-researchers will continue to leverage these tools, to explore new forms of expression and performance in virtual environments, collaborating closely with scientists. However, it is crucial to carefully examine the artistic access to the digital domain to ensure that the focus remains on creating genuine artworks rather than commercial products, thus maintaining the integrity of art creation.

AI generative music presents a fascinating intersection of technology and creativity, but it also raises significant ethical issues regarding musical authorship and intellectual property rights. AI's ability to compose music can democratize music creation, allowing individuals without formal training to produce high-quality compositions. However, traditional copyright laws are not well-equipped to handle works generated by non-human entities, leading to potential disputes over intellectual property. Additionally, there is the issue of originality and human artistry. AI systems often learn from existing music, which can blur the lines between inspiration and plagiarism. Furthermore, being automated systems, AI might be seen as replacing rather than augmenting human creativity. Balancing the benefits of AI generative music with these ethical considerations is crucial for ensuring that technological advancements enhance rather than undermine the cultural and artistic value of music. After the above mentioned worth-taking reflections on interactive technology and AI applications, it is needless to say that music creation and research is oriented to embrace new techno-aesthetic paradigms.

References

Antoniadis, P., Paschalidou, S., Duval, A., Jégo, J. F., & Bevilacqua, F. (2021). Rendering embodied experience into multimodal data: Concepts, tools, and applications for Xenakis' piano performance. *Xenakis 22: Centenary International Symposium*, Athens & Nafplio, Greece. https://hal.science/hal-03999834.

Blascovich, J., Loomis, J., Beall, A. C., Swinth, K. R., Hoyt, C. L., & Bailenson, J. N. (2002). Immersive virtual environment technology as a methodological tool for social psychology. *Psychological Inquiry,* 13, 103–124.

Born, G. (ed.) (2022). *Music and Digital Media: A Planetary Anthropology.* London: UCL Press (open access).

Born, G., J. Morris, F. Diaz & A. Anderson (2021). *Artificial Intelligence, Music Recommendation, and the Curation of Culture: A White Paper.* Toronto: Schwartz Reisman Institute for Technology and Society, University of Toronto.

Caruso, G. & Nijs, L. (2021) When Arts and Science meet, in *Journal of Music, Technology* (JMTE), Volume 13, Numbers 2-3, pp. 117-140(24).

Caruso, G. (2018). *Mirroring the intentionality and gesture of a piano performance : an interpretation of 72 Etudes Karnatiques, PhD Dissertation*, Ghent University Press. http://hdl.handle.net/1854/LU-8563258.

Caruso, G. (2024). Xr Music Performances in the Metaverse. Metaphase Project: A Case Study of a Phygital Piano Performance in Artistic Research in Music. *Journal of Artistic Research*, in publication.

Caruso, G., Coorevits, E., Nijs, L. & Leman, M. (2016). Gestures in Contemporary Music Performance: A Method to Assist the Performer's Artistic Process. In *Contemporary Music Review*, Volume 35, Issue 4-5: Gesture-Technology Interactions in Contemporary Music, pp. 402–422.

Caruso, G., Nijs, L., & Leman, M. (2021). "My avatar and me": technology-enhanced mirror in monitoring music performance practice, in Innovation in Music, Routledge, pp. 355 – 370.

De Assis, P., & Łukawski, A. (2024). *Decentralized music: Exploring blockchain for artistic research.* CRC Press.

Desmet, Franc – Nijs, Luc – Demey, Michiel – Lesaffre, Micheline – Martens, Jean-Pierre – Leman, Marc, *Assessing a Clarinet Player's Performer Textures in Relation to Locally Intended Musical Targets*, "Journal of New Music Research", vol. XLI/1 2012, pp. 31–48.

Goebel, W., Dixon, S., & Schubert, E. (2014). Quantitative methods: Motion analysis, audio analysis, and continuous response techniques. In D. Fabian, R. Timmers, & E. Schubert (Eds.), *Expressiveness in music performance: Empirical approaches across styles and cultures* (pp. 221-239). Oxford, UK: Oxford University Press.

Kyrlitsias, C., & Michael-Grigoriou, D. (2022). Social interaction with agents and avatars in immersive virtual environments: A survey. *Frontiers in Virtual Reality, 2*, 786665. https://doi.org/10.3389/frvir.2021.786665.

Leman, M., (2007), *Embodied Music Cognition and Mediation Technology*, MA: MIT Press, Cambridge.

Lesaffre, M., & Leman, M. (2020). Integrative research in art and science: a framework for proactive humanities. *Critical Arts-South-North Cultural An Media Studies, 34*(5), 39–54. https://doi.org/10.1080/02560046.2020.1788616.

Onderdijk, K. E., Bouckaert, L., Van Dyck, E., & Maes, P. J. (2023). Concert experiences in virtual reality environments. *Virtual Reality*, 1-14. https://doi.org/10.1007/s10055-023-00814-y.

Saunders, R., Gemeinboeck, P. (2022). Creative AI, Embodiment, and Performance. In Vear, C., Poltronieri, F. (eds) *The Language of Creative AI. Springer Series on Cultural Computing*. Springer, Cham. https://doi.org/10.1007/978-3-031-10960-7_11.

Schön, D. A. (1984). *The Reflective Practitioner: How Professionals Think in Action*. New York: Basic Books.

Schwab, M., & Borgdorff, H. (2014). *The Exposition of Artistic Research: Publishing Art in Academia*. Leiden: Leiden University Press.

Stillman, B. C. (2002). Making sense of proprioception: The meaning of proprioception, kinaesthesia and related terms. *Physiotherapy,* 88(11), 667-676. https://doi.org/10.1016/S0031-9406(05)60109-5.

Tanaka, A. (2010). Embodied musical interaction. In S. Holland, T. Mudd, K. Wilkie-McKenna, A. McPherson, & M. M. Wanderley (Eds.), *New Directions in Music and Human-Computer Interaction* (pp. 135-154). Cham, Switzerland: Springer.

Timmerman, K., & Vanoeveren, I. (2024). Empty mind: An exploration towards an autonomous digital experience and aesthetics within a virtual live performance. *Sixteenth International Conference on Tangible, Embedded, and Embodied Interaction* https://www.academia.edu/71882792/Empty_Mind_an_exploration_towards_an_autonomous_digital_experience_and_aesthetics_within_a_virtual_live_performance1.

Van Kerrebroeck, B., Caruso, G., & Maes, P.-J. (2021). A methodological framework for assessing social presence in music interactions in virtual reality. *Frontiers in Psychology,* 12. https://doi.org/10.3389/fpsyg.2021.663725.

Varela, F. J., Thompson, E., & Rosch, E. (2017). *The Embodied Mind: Cognitive Science and Human Experience*. Cambridge, MA: MIT Press Scholarship Online.

Wanderley, M. M., Vines, B. W. B., Middleton, N., McKay, C., & Hatch, W. (2005). The musical significance of clarinetists' ancillary gestures: An exploration of the field. *Journal of New Music Research, 34*(1), pp. 97-113.

Chapter 3

Synthesis: Interactive Intelligence

**Mario Spada
and Fabrizio Festa**[*]
Conservatoire E. R. Duni, Matera, Italy

Abstract

This chapter explores the synergistic potential of human intelligence and artificial intelligence in the context of the pinnacle of human endeavour—the creative act. Various forms of generative artificial intelligence (AI), i.e., ChatGPT, DALL-E, AIVA, Amper, Soundful, and Beatoven.ai, were combined with other software (Ableton Live, Blender) to create a storyline, 3D VR environments, and musical tracks. These are the core elements of an interactive live experience where the audience becomes integral to the creative process, making real-time selections to change the acoustic aenvironment and actively piloting the live electronics. Synthesis involves collaborative engagement, drawing on collective sensitivity and intelligence. It enables participation in a decision-making process shaped by shared and individual choices.

The individual response to collective choices is of particular interest since collective choices are unpredictable and may not necessarily involve a rational analysis of facts, which might be unknown to the participants. In this interactive live experience, the environments and events generated are unknown to the participants and are not bound by the physical laws or logic of the real world.

This approach explores the complexity of the decision-making process in shared experiences that invoke typical responses and behaviours linked to "Collective Intelligence."

---

[*] Corresponding Author's Email: f.festa@conservatoriomatera.it

In: Computational Arts and Creative Products
Editor: Alessandra Micalizzi
ISBN: 979-8-89530-426-6
© 2025 Nova Science Publishers, Inc.

Keywords: music, artificial intelligence, interactive intelligence

Introduction

The creation of intelligent machines has transformed our approach to life and science, leading to a profoundly fascinating path full of opportunities, and obstacles with much remaining to be explored. Insights, conflicts, surprises, and foresight have ushered in a new vision for humanity and our interactions with the environment, whether physical or virtual. The way we engage with machines has transformed significantly; they now efficiently address our needs by autonomously analysing information and learning from their interactions. Artificial neural networks (ANN), mathematical models with artificial neurons based on the biological functioning of the human brain, have played a leading role in this change. These networks consist of an interconnected information system that is fully adaptive and can modify its structure by analysing both external and internal data. Furthermore, we can create highly realistic and immersive three-dimensional environments with interactive features.

Reality can be imagined as a continuum, at one end lies the real environment, and at the other, the virtual environment, with mixed reality—comprising virtual and augmented reality—bridging the two. Virtual reality (VR) fully immerses users in a digital world, replacing the real world by stimulating multiple senses through sophisticated hardware and software, creating an entirely alternate virtual experience. It is a technology that uses a combination of hardware and software that, by deceiving two or more senses, creates a virtual world that replaces the real and tangible. It allows users to navigate photorealistic environments and interact with objects and users in real time.

Augmented reality (AR) operates on a different principle, relying on sensory perception that enhances the real world by overlaying digital content, thereby enriching reality with multiple levels of data. It is designed to maintain the user's connection to the real world. Synthesis was created by leveraging the capabilities of both virtual reality and augmented reality, harnessing their ability to dynamically interact with real-time events.

Sociological and Psychological Fundaments

The decision-making process is the constantly utilised primary cognitive function of humans. It is primarily driven by two motives: the desire to reduce uncertainty and the desire to gain an advantage. Consequently, the decision-making process is influenced not just by rationality but also by hedonic and emotional factors.

This century's experimental psychology has focused on emotions as a vehicle for decisions. Decisions manifest through brain activity as well as bodily responses to environmental stimuli. The decision-making process is the result of cognitive and emotional mental processes that allow and determine the selection of a line of action from various alternatives, leading to a definitive choice. This consideration of alternatives is influenced by recall of and comparison with past similar experiences. These memories are not neutral but rather characterised by emotions arising from positive or negative experiences. This is a deeply personal process; therefore, decision responses are not merely intellectual but also physical.

Effective decision making in complex social environments requires extensive knowledge and strategic thinking to successfully use that knowledge. Such decisions, known as social decisions, are intrinsically linked with survival. Consequently, all decision-making processes engage the entirety of the individual. The emotional process is an essential part of the neural system and its biological regulation. Decision-making involves intense brain activity, which involves several parallel tasks executed across various regions, and the thought process requires sustained mental representation. Human beings form neural representations that help us to predict outcomes and plan actions accordingly. Reflecting and deciding are particularly challenging, especially when one's existence and social context are at stake.

There is a clear distinction between personal and impersonal domains. The personal domain encompasses higher degrees of uncertainty and complexity. Decision-making within this domain is crucial for survival and becomes even more complex under time constraints. The decision-making process is complex and intrinsically linked to the individual called to make a choice. Everyone is characterised by their emotions and their relationship with the environment, their habits, and their social context. Emotions play a pivotal role in decision-making by altering the brain's physiological state. Choices involve interacting with the external environment and connecting with other individuals, leading to collective functioning. All choices are defined by experiences where an individual is embedded in a system of reality where all minds are linked. From this perspective, collective intelligence is an essential trait of human beings and crucial for the continuation of the species. In 1962, Douglas C. Engelbart defined collective intelligence as the ability of individuals to address problems and opportunities collaboratively and intelligently by harnessing collective perception, memory, insight, planning, thinking, foresight, and experience. He identifies the development of information technology as a means of fostering virtuous collaboration among individuals. Georg Pòr, in contrast, defines collective intelligence as the capability to evolve into higher complexity through innovation, leveraging the potential of differentiation, integration, competition, and collaboration. He states that only a community that constantly nourishes its intelligence can produce value for its members.

The philosopher Pierre Lèvy describes collective intelligence as a sociological phenomenon that can transform relationships and cultural diffusion. He believes collective intelligence has always existed since men have always been inclined to collaborate, creating synergies of skills in collective imagery, and storing competencies in collective memory. Languages, institutions, and techniques perfectly exemplify this osmotic effect between an individual and the community. This characteristic of humanity has evolved with modern technologies that eliminate distances and facilitate the sharing of records and competencies. Lèvy states that collective intelligence is a form of universally distributed intelligence that is constantly enhanced and coordinated in real time, effectively mobilising skills (Lèvy, 1994). For collective intelligence to exist, every individual must contribute skills that, in concert with the activity of other individuals, optimise and improve a virtuous system.

This process is supported by information technologies that enable the coordination of interactions in a virtual universe of knowledge. Mobilising knowledge implies acknowledging differences and highlighting the experiences of the individual. Collective intelligence is not static; it is a process of continuous evolution, not merely an accumulation of individual intelligence. As Aristoteles and Gestalt psychotherapists have stated, the whole is greater than the sum of its parts. Today's technological development allows one to create experiences in virtual and immersive environments, where it is possible to interact in real time with people from various locations all over the planet. Generating virtual experiences that transport an individual to new environments to be explored and understood fosters open-mindedness, self-recognition, and acknowledgement of one's abilities. It also presents a novel way of developing and sharing knowledge.

The Project

Synthesis is rooted in the context of assisted creativity, necessitating close cooperation with functional and accessible artificial intelligence.

The project was developed in four phases:

- Storyline generation and environmental design (ChatGPT-3)
- Creation of the environments via 3D modelling and VR optimisation (Craiyon, DALL-E 2, Blender, Vegas Pro, Photoshop, RX10)
- Generation of music (AIVA, Amper, Soundful, Beatoven.ai, Ableton Live)
- Design of the interactive live experience (Mentimeter, Ableton Live)

Storyline Generation and Environmental Design

The first phase of the project was initially conceived as a third-person narrative and involved the development of an interactive story/plot. The plot unfolds with a child as the main character who has found a carillon that, when played, reveals that the world the character is in is a simulation/virtual world.

ChatGPT-3 was used to develop the plot and the text prompt contained all necessary information (Figure 1, Figure 2). Three scenarios were requested, each offering two distinct alternatives for plot development. The first option describing an AI-generated forest in which everything is interconnected was selected and used for further development. Subsequently, two additional alternatives were requested.

Option 3, describing a lake with marine creatures, and Option 4, where the protagonist decides to follow a glowing trail, were selected by participants to further develop the storyline.

Subsequently, participants selected the option to shift the setting of the story to a futuristic city. As the story continued to unfold, participants opted to change from a third-person narrative to a first-person narrative. However, the third-person narrative was still used for interactions with ChatGPT. The AI-generated concept of a journey through space was chosen for further exploration.

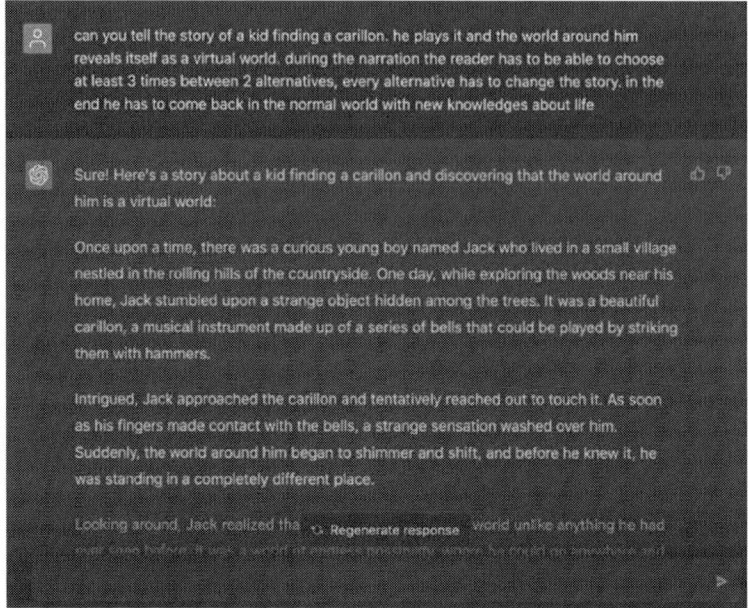

Figure 1. An example of interaction with ChatGPT-3.

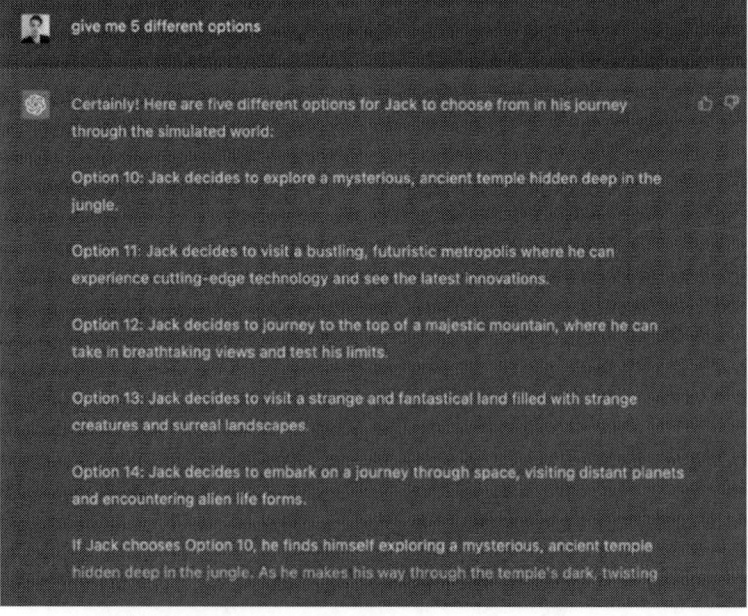

Figure 2. An example of interaction with ChatGPT-3.

Participants specified that the main character should journey through environments representing supervised, unsupervised, and reinforcement learning. Although the initial results were intriguing, a new prompt was necessary to specify focusing on environment creation rather than the introduction of new characters.

The AI-generated option for unsupervised learning was appealing to participants, who requested a desert setting. The resulting image was considered suitable for further development of the storyline The final prompt was based on the usage of punch cards in the context of the Analytical Engine developed by Charles Babbage. The result, interpreting the Analytical Engine as a primitive form of supervised learning, was the final selection. With the selection of AI-generated options completed, the focus of the audience participation switched to the creation of 3D environments.

The selected scenes, with their respective assigned titles, were as follows:

1. Room - Corridor
2. Interconnected Forest - ReGeneration
3. Lake - Underwater
4. Futuristic City - Noise Temple
5. Light Trail - Game Place
6. Space - Neural Space
7. Desert - Unsupervised Grains
8. Analytical Engine - Engine

Creation of the Environments, 3D Modelling, and VR Optimization

Text-to-image artificial intelligence was used to create the scenes, specifically Craiyon and DALL-E 2, which are both transformer neural networks. The prompt for the initial scene, "Corridor", was: slender figure of a monster in a dark corridor. The images generated led to a different prompt: alien in a dark corridor. One of the images generated by Craiyon (Figure 3) was used as a graphical reference for the final 3D model (Figure 4). In this scene, the alien figure standing at the end of the hallway leads the main character to two doors, one marked with a "0" and the other with "1". Both doors open to a virtual world, symbolising the link between the decision-making process and the digital dimension.

Figure 3. Image generated by Craiyon for scene "Corridor."

Figure 4. "Corridor" final 3D model.

Figure 5. Image generated by Craiyon for scene "ReGeneration."

Figure 6. "ReGeneration" final 3D model.

In scene 2, "ReGeneration", ChatGPT was prompted to describe a setting with a lush forest where everything is interconnected. That resulted in an environment with luminescent vegetation and light orbs. The prompt was: a forest with luminescent plants and light orbs. One of the images generated by Craiyon (Figure 5) was used as a graphical reference for the final 3D model (Figure 6). In the script, the entire planet participates in the creation of a new plant, an entity born from the energy of the surrounding matter. That entity controls, together with the other plants, the existence of the planet itself. This references the idea of collective intelligence and interconnection between individuals.

In scene 3, "Unsupervised Grains", the interaction with ChatGPT led to an environment symbolising Unsupervised Learning. The prompt was: a desert with a night sky of circuits realistic. An image generated by Craiyon (Figure 7) from this prompt was used as a graphical reference for the final 3D model (Figure 8).

The scene depicts a neural network that functions similarly to the human brain. Its neural connections, facilitate independent classification and identification of features and patterns.

Figure 7. Image generated by Craiyon for scene "Unsupervised Grains".

Synthesis: Interactive Intelligence   35

Figure 8. "Unsupervised Grains" final 3D model.

Scene 4, "Underwater", was generated from the following prompt: a lake delimited by circuits with sea creatures like jellyfish and fish digital art. One of the images generated by DALL-E 2 (Figure 9) was used as a graphical reference for the 3D model (Figure 10).

The scene depicted biological and mechanical beings functioning together, respecting a shared environment. A motherboard and a power adapter float over the water; these control the environment. An old PC lies on the sandy ground, and its screen broadcasts a video about Sensorama, the first technological artefact that led to the creation of modern VR systems.

Interactions with ChatGPT for scene 5, Noise Temple, resulted in the creation of a virtual simulation of a futuristic city inspired by the stable diffusion model. The prompt was: a futuristic city in the eighties virtual reality. One of the generated images was selected (Figure 11), and the style for the 3D model was adapted to mimic the aesthetic of the first VR simulation (Figure 12). In the story, the main character is led through an unfinished cityscape and arrives at a crossroads where the image of a temple, created from noise, appears.

Figure 9. Image generated by DALL-E 2 for scene "Underwater."

Figure 10. "Underwater" final 3D model.

Figure 11. Image generated by Craiyon for scene "Noise Temple."

Figure 12. "Noise Temple" final 3D model.

Figure 13. Image generated by Craiyon for scene "Game Place."

Figure 14. "Game Place" final 3d model.

In scene 6, Game Place, the interaction with ChatGPT suggested the idea of gaming as a structure of entertainment that allows new experimentation, creating new social and technological opportunities. The prompt used was: dark geometric videogame ambient with glowing trail. One of the images generated (Figure 13) has been used as a graphical reference for the final 3D model (Figure 14). The scene's environment is characterised by a large screen broadcasting the gameplay of Tennis For Two, the first-ever videogame. As the plot unfolds, lines in the background begin to fade as though the virtual gaming world is merging with reality.

Neural Space (scene 7) was based on prompting ChatGPT to describe a journey through space. Participants decided to enquire about the functioning of a multilayer perceptron. The prompt used was: planets in space in the shape of an artificial neural network. Figure 15 shows the image that was used to create the 3D model in Figure 16.

In scene 8, entitled Engine, interaction with ChatGPT led to an exploration of the underlying concept of the Analytical Engine and its punch cards. The prompt used was: a dark room made by gears. One of the images generated (Figure 17) has been used as a graphical reference for the final 3D model (Figure 18).

Figure 15. Image generated by Craiyon for scene "Neural Space."

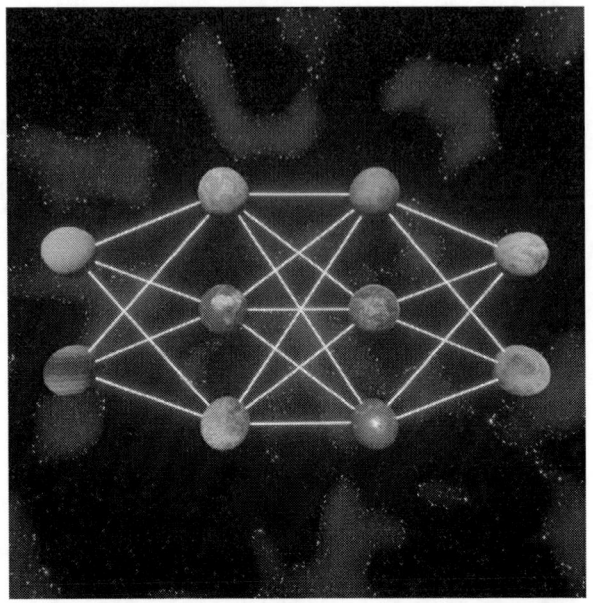

Figure 16. "Neural Space" final 3D model.

Figure 17. Image generated by Craiyon for scene "Engine."

Figure 18. "Engine" final 3D model.

A perforated punch card is at the centre of the scene. The card enters the gears and exits with lines of binary code that have replaced the original holes. This emphasises the connection between old and modern technology.

All the 3D models and their animations were created in collaboration with the digital artist Boris Pietrocola, using Blender and Vegas Pro 19.

Generation of Music

The music tracks for this project were all developed through interactions with AI music generators. The AI music generator Amper Music, now defunct, was used for the music track for "Corridor." The environment evoked mystery, fear, and discovery. The parameters used for the generation of this track were: cinematic ambient, mysterious, key G, 2–3 min. The AI tool used the following instruments: synth, pad, piano, strings, textures, and a 20-inch suspended cymbal. Effects such as reverb and delay were added to every instrument. When the audio track was generated, it was segmented, manipulated, and enhanced to create audio samples. Pads and audio special effects were also added.

Pitching, reverb, delay, granulation, reverse, panning, and EQ were all utilised in the creation of the music tracks. The AI music generator Soundful was used for the music track "Game Place." The parameters were: moods & themes, technology, 3 min, 124 bpm, key Dm. The audio track was cut and processed to create a drone sound. Other parts of the audio tracks were used to create audio effects and pads. Audio samples, glitch drums, and textures were used in the final track. The AI music generator AIVA was used for the music track "Noise Temple." The parameters were: cyberpunk ambient, 2–3 min, essential, CM, one composition. The generated audio track, which was cut and reversed, has been processed to create a drone sound. Sounds and audio samples were dynamically added to the drone in the final track. The AI music generator AIVA was also used for the music track "Unsupervised Grains." The parameters were: reflective atmosphere, 2:30–3 min, key F#M. The generated track was segmented into four parts. The first was processed and used to create a drone sound. The second was doubled, reversed, and processed through a chorus, creating another drone sound. The third was cut, reversed, and used within the central part of the final track. The fourth was cut, reversed, processed through audio effects, and used for the end of the final track. The AI music generator Soundful was used to create the music track for "Neural Space." The parameters were: ambient, 90 bpm, critical AM, 6–8 min. The generated audio track was cut to reduce the timing and used with other drone sounds and samples for the final track. The music track entitled "ReGeneration" was created by the AI music generator Beatoven.ai.

The parameters were: 3 min, ambient, triumphant. One part of this AI-generated soundtrack was used to create the repeated sound of the central segment of the final track. Another section of the track was processed and used to create a drone sound. Additional samples and textures were cut, processed, reversed, equalised, and panned in the final track. "Underwater" was another creation with Soundful. The parameters were: ambient, mood and themes, meditation, 100bpm, Em. The equalised output was used. One part of the track was cut and processed through Ableton Live Redux. Audio samples, reverb, and panning were used in the final track. The final track "Engine" was also composed with Soundful. Here, the parameters were: moods & themes, hype beats, 135 bpm, and key FM. Three parts of the track were selected, processed, and used to create a drone sound, percussive sounds, and a pad. These audio samples were processed and used in the final track.

All tracks were mixed and mastered under the supervision of the mix and master engineer, Dario Logallo, using Ableton Live 11 and Reaper 6.78. Scores were visualised using the AI-driven tool Craiyon, All the scores were

Synthesis: Interactive Intelligence 43

designed in collaboration with the architect and designer Erika Nolè using Photoshop 24.2.1 and Izotope RX10.3. When the music tracks were completed, they were added to the 3D videos and uploaded to YouTube. At the end of every video, the user was allowed to choose between options that lead to different environments. The decision paths for these interactions with the virtual world are illustrated in the decision tree in Figure 19.

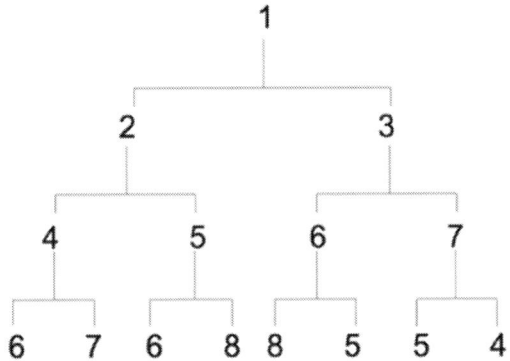

Figure 19. "Synthesis" Decision tree.

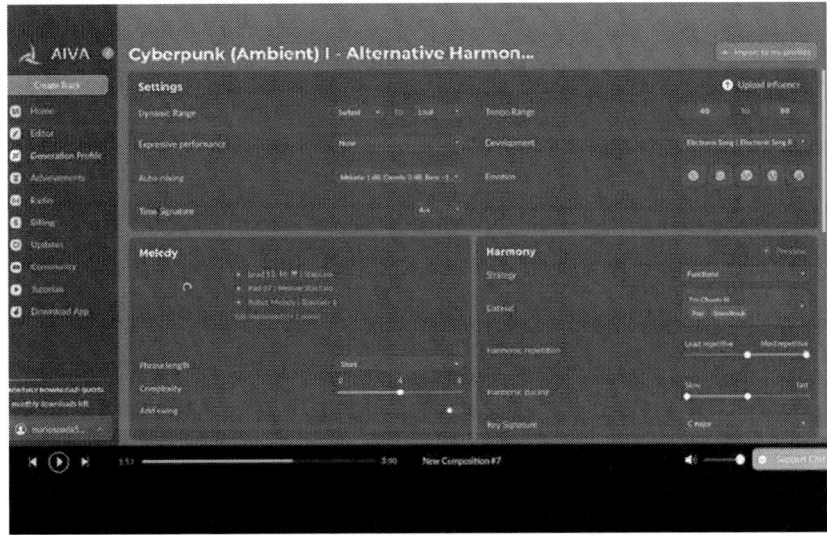

Figure 20. An example of the interface of an AI music generator (in this case, AIVA).

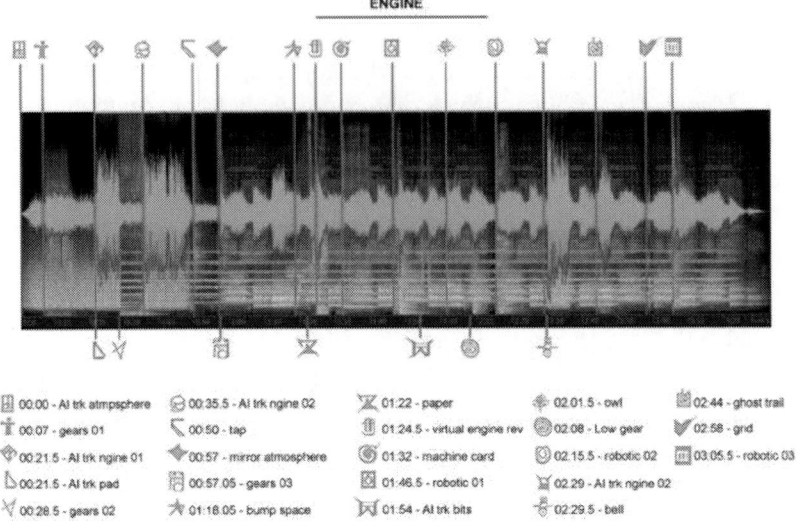

Figure 21. An example of a score, in this case for the music track "Engine."

In the development of the decision tree a number was assigned to each scene using the following scheme:

1. Corridor
2. Game Place
3. Noise Temple
4. Unsupervised Grains
5. Neural Space
6. ReGeneration
7. Underwater
8. Engine

Designing the Interactive Live Experience

All music tracks generated for Synthesis were used to create the live experience. Each track represents a specific environment and can be manipulated in a live session. The experience begins with the Corridor sound environment, where the audience is given the power to direct the development of the sound path, actively piloting the live music session. The online tool Mentimeter, accessible via QR Code, directs the audience to a real-time survey where participants choose between two images depicting different environments. There is a 15-second time limit for voting.

The sound environment selected by the majority of participants dictates the direction of the live music session. This, coupled with improvisation from the musicians, ensures the uniqueness of each sound path.

Conclusion

Reality and virtuality are becoming increasingly intertwined, transforming our perceptions and interactions with the world. The art world is experiencing a profound shift. Collaborating with artificial intelligence in creating works of art is a unique experience that opens novel avenues for engagement and exploration. From generating sounds to interacting with the environment, Synthesis aims to find a new process of making art. In this way, human intelligence is strictly linked to artificial intelligence in a highly dynamic dimension.

References

Boden M. A., *Intelligenza artificiale*, Il Mulino, Bologna, 2019.
Damasio, A. R. et al. *L'errore di Cartesio: emozione, ragione e cervello umano*, Adelphi, Milano, 1994.
Damasio H. Damasio A. R. Lee G. P., Different contributions of the human amygdala and ventromedial prefrontal cortex to decision-making, *Journal of Neuroscience*, 19, Society for Neuroscience, 1999, pp. 5473–5481.
Engelbart D. C., *Workstation History and The Augmented Knowledge Workshop*, McDonnell Douglas Corp., ACM Conference on the History of Personal Workstations, Palo Alto, 1986.
Levy P., *L'Intelligenza Collettiva: Per un'Antropologia del Cyberspazio*, Feltrinelli, Milano, 2002.
Pòr G., *The Quest for Collective Intelligence*, New Leaders Press, 1995.
Young J. Z., *I filosofi e il cervello*, Bollati Boringhieri, Torino, 2017.

Chapter 4

Something Like Orpheus: Using AI to Make New Music to Hear the Past

Alessandro Ratoci[1,*]
and Clemence Martel[2,†]

[1]Departement of Jazz and New Technologies,
Conservatorio di Musica Lucio Campiani, Mantova, Italy
2Independent artist and researcher, Paris, France

Abstract

According to R. Murray Schafer, the inventor of sound ecology, the myth of Orpheus, and his instrument, the lyre, represents one of the earliest attempts to connect scientific knowledge to art. In pursuit of this ideal, this work explores the integration of artificial intelligence (AI) with historical music repertoires, attempting to unite human creativity and machine learning in mixed music compositions. Using Monteverdi's *L'Orfeo* (1607) as a foundation, the project reimagines classical forms through the lens of AI, preserving the central role of human creativity while employing computational techniques to generate novel soundscapes. This chapter examines the workflows, tools, and aesthetic outcomes of these processes, offering insights into how AI can act as a co-creative partner in contemporary composition.

Keywords: artificial creativity, human-machine collaboration, mixed music, computer-assisted composition, tibre transfer, Orpheus mythology

---

[*] Corresponding Author's Email: alessandro.ratoci@conservatoriomantova.com
[†] Corresponding Author's Email: martelclemence@gmail.com

In: Computational Arts and Creative Products
Editor: Alessandra Micalizzi
ISBN: 979-8-89530-426-6
© 2025 Nova Science Publishers, Inc.

What Orpheus Is, and What It Isn't

We combine the perspectives of both the composer and the performer within the specific practice of mixed music. The selected works, *Something Like Orpheus/Something Like Eurydice*-for a variable number of human performers and live electronics - exemplifies, through its realization process, a symbiotic approach that merges the paradigms of "natural" human-centered creativity and "artificial" computer-centered generation. By emphasizing the interplay between human and digital agents as a distinct aesthetic trait, mixed music is particularly well-suited for reflecting on the convergence of "natural" and "artificial" creative approaches.

Which Orpheus?

The piece draws on the historically rich myth of Orpheus, particularly through Claudio Monteverdi's seminal early Baroque opera *L'Orfeo* (1607). The connection with the original *Orfeo* involves both symbolic (musical notation) and sonic (audio recordings) media, compiled into a corpus that includes public domain and commercial recordings, MIDI files, and scores. Employing corpus-based techniques alongside algorithmic methods to reinterpret this material is in keeping with practices commonly associated with artificial creativity (Manaris 2007) (Schwarz 2007).

This chapter is aimed at a multidisciplinary audience who may not be music experts but are curious about the artist's perspective on their work. Therefore, we will describe the general workflow, including the tools used and methods of integrating them (Wishart 1994), the associations with elements of the work's poetics, and an evaluation of the results in aesthetic terms.

The research does not extensively explore the development of new tools; rather, it focuses on integrating existing ones with concepts and techniques from compositional tradition - such as notation - and electroacoustic practices. It examines how these integrations can offer a robust technical foundation for creating innovative yet cohesive aesthetics.

Essentially, this chapter aims to establish potential connections between digital technologies, historical repertoires, and the expression of a novel, original poetics. It seeks to offer a valuable situation that showcases the interplay between the AI and musicians' perceptual filters, thought structures, and operational frameworks. By focusing on a specific experience that highlights generalizable traits, it seeks to provide insights into how creatives use artificial intelligence tools and why they are inclined to do so.

A Safe Distance from Historical Models

"Something Like Orpheus/Eurydice" was chosen because it reveals a unique potential of generative AI music tools: the ability to transform iconic elements from classical and popular musical traditions by freeing these elements from their cultural and historical burdens. As these transformations occur mostly without human input, the process mimics a kind of "lost and found" dynamic where the composer re-encounters distorted remnants of familiar objects. Through digital "degradation," these sources are revitalized and become fertile once more as sources of inspiration.

By incorporating artificial agents into the workflow, a distance is created between the creator and the models that may have unconsciously influenced the composer's imagination. This approach also liberates the composer from the aura, sacrality, and perceived untouchability of historical masterworks. The process seeks to avoid the risk of these elements becoming clichés, fueled by a utopian desire to recapture a fresh, innocent, and wonder-filled perspective.

Orpheus' Ancestors

The present project is part of a larger cycle that shares a consistent approach toward pre-existing materials. Over the course of about ten years, this cycle has explored diverse artifacts and repertoires, along with various cultural mechanisms and methodologies, all variously connected to the composer's personal experiences and cultural development.

The exploration started with the personal ethnomusicological heritage and identity - the "Ottava Rima" Tuscan singing tradition - as reinterpreted in *Rima-Flow* for tuba and fixed media (Ratoci 2016). The subject of transformation was then applied to another popular culture - the African American tradition - with *East St. Louis Blues* for piano and live electronics in 2018. The approach was then extended to the noise-rock style of Sonic Youth, exemplified in *Confused Idols and Sexy Killers* for electric guitar and computer, where a database-centered workflow for symbolic music transformations was also employed (Ratoci 2020). Finally, drawing from the classical background, it was time to apply the same approach to rework an important piece of classical music culture, and that is the present case with the opera *L'Orfeo* by Claudio Monteverdi.

Orpheus as a Whole

"Something Like..." is an open musical form that offers flexibility in both its structure and the number and types of participating musicians. It serves as a dynamic platform where various performers - vocalists and instrumentalists - act as interpreters and improvisers.

Envisioned as a loose interpretation of the remix concept, the work extensively reworks the instrumental and vocal pieces from Monteverdi's original opera. Through style and genre transfer, these elements shift from their early Baroque style and language to the patterns of contemporary experimental mixed music.

Rather than attempting to reconstruct the complete narrative of the original opera, the project aims to emulate a collection of remnants - similar to partially erased recordings that have been recovered and replayed through a malfunctioning or incompatible decoding system. This system does not faithfully translate the material; instead, it disrupts, reinvents, destroys, and recreates a faint (or occasionally vivid) echo of the original work.

Orpheus and Eurydice

In Striggio and Monteverdi's operatic narrative, the tale of Orpheus is the omnipresent and almost overwhelming presence in the drama, while Eurydice is but an evanescent echo, rising to the role of solo voice only twice, for few minutes in an opera spanning nearly two hours.

This rendition retells the story of Orpheus from the viewpoint of the female co-protagonist, who assumes the role of the human, or more precisely, the "trans-human" presence. Orpheus becomes a significant yet absent figure, manifesting only in a "disembodied" form through the instruments and electronics. In contrast to Orpheus's absent humanity, Eurydice embodies a multifaceted persona - simultaneously human, trans-human, and monster. She shifts from being the song's object to becoming its subject, transformed into a magical being by Orpheus's music.

Eurydice as Voice and Body

In the tradition of classical antiquity and in the opera itself, Orpheus, to win over Eurydice, manages to "move" the inanimate elements of nature - stones, animals, and finally the monstrous creatures of the underworld - both physically and emotionally.

Eurydice, utilizing tools provided by artificial intelligence, is able to manipulate the sonic essence of various elements: the concrete sounds of minerals, atmospheric elements, animal vocalizations, and even generate entirely new timbres of imaginary monstrous creatures.

Thanks to timbre transfer techniques based on variational autoencoder (VAE) technology (Caillon et Esling 2021), Eurydice sometimes appears as a solo voice, sometimes as a choir, and at other times as the spirit animating inanimate objects.

The manipulation of sonic features transfers onto the voice, the symbol of Eurydice's body, embodying Orpheus's desire represented by the countless entities that his song awakens in the legend.

An Exploratory Approach

When we engage with a significant figure from the repertoire, such as Eurydice - whether as interpreters, performers, or composers - a multitude of reflective layers opens up beyond the purely musical aspect. These layers include the semantic value of the text and the way it is conveyed through sound - in short, how the story is told.

As we perceived the digital tools as a sort of "revelator," prior to viewing them as instruments meant to produce and shape the material that would eventually be solidified in the final work, we introduced an additional step during the preparatory phase: we enjoyed manipulating, tampering with, and disrupting all the parameters that define Eurydice's voice. All this work on pitch, speed, timbre, texture, and diction was done without expectations or preconceived ideas. This made it possible to reveal vastly different versions of Eurydice, one after another, sometimes even to the brink of absurdity.

This phase of experimentation enabled us to engage in what we might call a work of "subtraction." All these figures that did not originate from our own imagination served as dissonances against which we could react, rebel, or embrace. By continually responding to these machine-generated distortions with the recurring phrase, "...look! I didn't see her like that!," we eventually ended up "seeing her" and "having her." This play on words echoes Lacanian concepts - *la voir* (to see her) and *l'avoir* (to have her).

Yet Another Eurydice

"We become ourselves only through the trial of the Other."[1]

Confronting ourselves with this multitude of external incarnations of Eurydice has given birth to "our" Eurydice. By challenging our preconceptions and dismantling established icons, digital tools have enabled us to give birth to such an imaginary entity. Thanks to this process, which remains highly subjective, Eurydice is transformed from the figure of a specter rooted in a narrative constructed since Antiquity to that of a fantasy - an object imbued with our own imagination and intimacy.

Eurydice: Fantasy or Monster?

In many narratives, Eurydice is presented almost exclusively through her relationship with Orpheus. This narrative gap - this emptiness and apparent transparency, this elusive quality - allows both the artist and the spectator to project themselves intensely and completely onto her. With her, there is a much stronger emotional and symbolic resonance than with many other characters.

Moreover, by virtue of her theatrical role, we are all potential Eurydice. Like her, we are all beings in waiting. We all explore our dependence on the "Other" and grapple with the tension between idealizing the object of our desire and confronting the immobility of that perfect image, often unattainable in reality.

Consequently, we felt the need to free Eurydice from the archetype of the immobile woman, eternally waiting - a concept so aptly depicted by Roland Barthes in *A Lover's Discourse* (Barthes 1978)

"Am I in love? - Yes, because I'm waiting. The other never waits. Sometimes I want to play the part of one who doesn't wait; I try to busy

---

[1] Maurice Merleau-Ponty: "Nous ne devenons nous-mêmes que par l'épreuve de l'Autre." (Merleau-Ponty 1945).

myself elsewhere, to arrive late; but I always lose at this game: whatever I do, I find myself there, with nothing to do, punctual, even ahead of schedule. The lover's fatal identity is nothing more than: I am the one who waits."

Eurydice of the Thousand Voices

We have made Eurydice a character with a thousand voices and a thousand faces. All the different voices that have taken on this role will come to inhabit the singer's mouth in turn - a kind of fantastic Hydra, a Protean being capable of taking the form of each of us. This serves as a reincarnation of her universality and the anthropological invariant she personifies desire; in other words, a perfect monster (from the Latin *monstrare,* to show).

In its ancient meaning, a *monstrum* is a supernatural being with unusual forms sent by the gods to reveal to humans a form of alterity that defies norms and challenges us about our own nature and the mysteries of the universe.

Here, Eurydice as the monster becomes a powerful symbol of the universality of the profound human longing that runs through her. Whether viewed as a monster or a transhumanist fantasy, we take the liberty of remaining undecided, embracing this ambiguity. Since her function lies in the realm of sound, the voice is the only organ that can be modified without surgery. For her transformation, we instead employed a rich palette of digital sound processing (DSPs).

Orpheus and Nature: The Average Composer's Deal with Artificial Creativity

Recent studies have observed that the proliferation of computer-based tools in language, visual arts, and music has led to a new form of the creative process known as "artificial creativity" (Moruzzi 2021).

Despite being a trending term among artists and festival curators, the concept of "artificial creativity" still lacks a clear definition and measurable criteria. Some studies, (Runco 2023) question whether artificial creativity can be considered genuine creativity when compared to traditional views of the creative process while other (Esling et Devis 2020) adopt a more possibilist perspective, focusing on the advancements needed for artificial tools to seamlessly integrate into human creative processes.

Orpheus versus the Machine

One possible reason for the difficulty in clearly defining "artificial creativity" may stem from contrasting it with "natural creativity," the mechanisms and exclusively anthropocentric nature of which are still debated in neuropsychology. Despite this theoretical uncertainty, over the past 20 years, music composers have progressively integrated computer-centered tools into their daily work, transforming their poetics and aesthetics in the direction informed by these new instruments.

This raises the question of whether this theoretical framework is truly adequate to describe what creators think about the tools they use and the processes they engage with, and whether the dichotomy between natural and artificial really applies from the author's perspective at the moment the work is conceived and crafted. The power of any creative technology lies in its potential to enable the creator to express an idea through its use, while still considering the result as their own artifact and not merely a product of the tool. In simple terms, the medium must possess a certain degree of transparency to allow the author to identify with their works, and vice versa.

A Question About Authorship

The rise of AI tools that rely on pre-trained models challenges the traditional notion of authorship. Who is the 'author' of a piece created with AI assistance? Is it the artist who uses the tool, the developers who created the model, or the numerous anonymous contributors whose data trained the model? These questions are not merely theoretical but have significant legal and ethical implications. For example, recent debates in the visual arts have questioned whether AI-generated images infringe on copyright if they draw from a database of existing works. In music, this concern is equally relevant, especially when the training of AI models is based on iconic classical pieces like Monteverdi's "L'Orfeo."

Artists seem to navigate these seemingly overwhelming questions by forging their own paths through the theoretical complexities of digital creativity, focusing on what these technologies offer in terms of speed and quality. While generally trained in human-centered creativity, many artists have recently developed methods to seamlessly integrate new technologies, often termed "disruptive," into their workflows.

This integration enables them to maintain a consistent output while embracing a long-term vision of evolution and change. This is possible only by imagining a functional continuity, an ergonomic fusion between traditional means of natural creativity and artificial intelligence-informed ones.

Natural and Artificial Continuity

Our goal is to evolve our vision of the work while ensuring the production of viable outputs, essential for fostering growth while remaining faithful to past experiences. Furthermore, we reject a labor-centered view of authorship, wherein the connection to one's work is measured by the amount of effort expended.

We assert that the quality and value of artistic creation are not inherently tied to the quantity of labor involved. Rather, the appraisal of artistic merit should be based on its ability to convey meaning, evoke emotions, and engage audiences effectively.

By decoupling artistic value from labor metrics, we emphasize the importance of creativity, innovation, and the intrinsic qualities of the work itself. This perspective recognizes that impactful art can emerge from both intensive labor and streamlined processes, highlighting the fact that efficiency and conceptual depth are equally, if not more, critical to artistic success.

The Power of Identification

For this reason, it is more insightful to measure the connection between the author and their tools not in quantitative terms (i.e., assessing how much or how little a tool actually assists the composer in producing their music) but rather in terms of its potential to identify. This concept involves evaluating the extent to which a tool enables the human agent to perceive the resulting work as an extension of their personal artistic approach and identity. Even when the bulk of labor-intensive, time-consuming tasks are performed by the machine, the tool's ability to resonate with the user's unique creative vision remains essential.

Furthermore, this framework challenges the traditional separation between human creativity and machine efficiency. It suggests that meaningful artistic expression can emerge from the harmonious integration of automated processes and human intentionality. By recognizing and valuing the potential of tools in terms of identifiability, we open up avenues for innovative collaborations between humans and technology, where one enhances the other's strengths. This paradigm not only helps to redefine and clarify authorship in the digital age but also broadens our understanding of creativity as a dynamic interplay between the artist and their chosen instruments.

The Tradition of Computer Aided Composition

Computer aided (or assisted) composition (CAC) techniques have held a steady place in the formative curriculum of Western composers since the establishment of the IRCAM Cursus in 1980 (Robert 2021). This curriculum includes techniques and real-life examples of a formalized approach to music composition, developed by well-established composers during IRCAM's pioneering phase of artistic research.

In this now widely adopted tradition, formalization represents a crystallization of human-centered reflection and operation. Composers learn to create formalized musical processes manually, using immediate tools such as paper and pencil. Once they understand the impact of these methods on their aesthetic outcomes, the task of automation - through generalization and repetition - is delegated to the computer. One notable example of this workflow is illustrated in detail through Brian Fernyhough's techniques for melody and rhythm generation in the OpenMusic language (Malt 2006).

Many composers are thus familiar with the concept of formalizing and automating creative processes, though primarily in the context of replicating human-generated workflows. By delegating the fabrication of elements to automated processes - only after their prototypes have been painstakingly hand-crafted - composers maintain the impression that the computer's output remains an integral part of their artistic craft.

Navigating the Parametric Space

A similar situation arises in electroacoustic composition, where computers are used as tools for the synthesis or manipulation of concrete sounds. As extensively explored by musicologists, composers and sound artists (Emmerson 1982) (Wishart 1994) (Barret 1997) (Landy 2019), the primary means to impose a creative intent and predict the outcome of such operations is to navigate a parametric space.

By navigating this parametric space, composers can make informed decisions and accurately anticipate the machine's results, thereby effectively utilizing the computer for its designated tasks. In this space, aural results are associated with numerical parameter values, with the resulting sound considered an intersection point of these dimensions. This approach allows composers to understand and control the relationship between the parameters and the resulting sonic characteristics.

All a Game of Chance

In the field of music composition, we consider "traditional" an approach in which the composer tightly controls every aspect of the outcome in a deterministic manner, embodying a meticulous organization of sound materials reminiscent of the Romantic and Beethovenian visions of the creator. Conversely, we define the indeterminate methodology as one that embraces an open-ended and unpredictable workflow, incorporating aleatory and indeterminacy concepts that allow chance and randomness to influence the parameters to varying degrees. This shift, influenced by the European and American avant-garde movements of the 1960s, has introduced a new dimension to the craft of musical composition.

While this deterministic approach continues to be employed, new paradigms based on controlled *alea* offer composers an alternative means to foster creativity, enabling them to navigate a parametric space where chance and deliberate manipulation coexist. This duality allows composers to maintain structured control while also incorporating elements of unpredictability, thereby expanding the possibilities of musical expression.

Different proportions of randomness in musical processes have long been integral to computer tools for sound manipulation, ranging from the most obscure to the mainstream. These tools have consistently served to introduce elements of surprise or variability into otherwise static workflows, offering unexpected solutions or even overcoming momentary lapses in inspiration.

A Gradual Adaptation

While the aleatory characteristics inherent in traditional sound transformation and synthesis structurally differ from those of artificial intelligence tools, they have, to some extent, familiarized composers with a workflow in which the interaction between human operator and machine can be inverted. The creative process does not rely solely on human input; rather, it can also be influenced or significantly inspired by the outputs of autonomous machine generation.

A specific category of tools that extensively utilize randomization can be classified as "black boxes." In these software tools, the user solely provides input to the system (typically a sound file), and the tool functions as an autonomous transformer or generator with no further user intervention beyond the initial input. These tools, usually available as freeware, gained popularity within the experimental and IDM music scenes during the late 1990s and are situated within the broader framework of generative music. Although these tools are based on more "traditional" algorithms (e.g., granular synthesis, FFT), they necessitate an explorative approach from the user akin to that employed when working with one of the most widely used neural network-based tools for audio transformation and generation, the variational autoencoder (VAEs).

Variational autoencoder (Kingma 2013) (Cinelli, et al. 2021) (Caillon et Esling 2021) (Takale, Mahalle et Sule 2024) are a type of neural network model often used in image and sound transformation. These models encode input data into a compressed latent representation, which is then decoded back into its original domain.

In audio processing VAEs are a type of machine learning model that allows for the manipulation of sound by encoding its key attributes, such as pitch and timbre, into a latent space. From there, these sounds can be altered or combined to generate entirely new outputs. In the composition of *" Something Like Orpheus / Something Like Eurydice"* various approaches have been integrated into a unified workflow. This includes the careful fine-tuning of parameters, experimentation with "black boxes," and trial-and-error exploration of latent neural spaces. These methods converge in the effort to transform a stylistically and historically significant repertoire, drawing inspiration for the creation of new music.

The Magical Black Box

In the "Black Box" paradigm, the creator's only means of control is through the selection of input material. This choice becomes pivotal in establishing a personal and causal connection between the creator and the artifact ("I made this!"), as it is the sole point of interaction between the author's intent and the final output. Within the terminology of the acousmatic music tradition, the composer relinquishes control over the intrinsic qualities of the sound - those purely articulative and concrete properties such as timbre, rhythm, and pitch. As a result, the only characteristic that can be expected to persist is the extrinsic one: the sonic identity of the input material, provided it remains unchanged and "resists" transformation.

This approach is particularly effective for genres like soundscape and ambient music, which emphasize broad, dramatic development over intricate microforms, such as rhythmic loops or grooves. It is also highly suitable for generating background elements (pads, textures, etc.) that serve as a foundation for more prominent musical articulations.

The Mindless Orpheus of Background Music

A particularly strange and intriguing example of audio software, based on the black box principle, is **thOnk_0+2** (second version) by AudioEase (1996–1998). This half-obscure gem was employed specifically to craft background sonorities that are non-intrusive yet distinctively recognizable and well-characterized. The user interface of **thOnk_0+2** proclaims:

> "thOnk provides the sonic treasure-chest composers can turn to harvest fresh, unanticipated, highly narrative material. Without having to think at all."

Despite being developed by what would later become a prominent commercial software house, the software was released as freeware and can still be run on modern computers via Classic MacOS 9.0.4 emulation. Although lacking user-tweakable parameters, it compensates with a carefully curated set of presets. These presets are so thoughtfully designed that they transform the software into a small piece of textual art, infused with the characteristic English humor associated with the early days of the IDM music scene:

"Classic Flowing: from the original ThOnk, provides slowly evolving narrative mini compositions. Try 10 seconds of hi-density fast paced input/Classic Hectic: from the original ThOnk, moves around fast. You can clip short events from the output for FX samples. Give it hot leveled audio/Pentathon: gives a two voice, brownian walk, pentatonic counterpoint. Feed it one note or a very short melody for solid tonal results/Shepard: Roger Shepard invented circular pitch. This stream keeps going down in micro and macro pitch and in speed / Slack: Slack is not the hand of God. Slack, is the way the wind swirls, and the dust settles, eons after God has passed by. (K. Vonnegut, The Sirens of Titan, 1959) Ztochaztlk = akadem!k wank (sic!), etc."

For each section within the musical work, the algorithm was assigned its respective "complementary" sound. For instance, in sections dominated by saxophone, the background layers were derived from samples of the vocal parts, and conversely, vocal sections drew their background from saxophone samples. This methodological approach employs the indeterminate principles to generate intricate and evolving granular sound streams based on the provided samples. The tool reliably produces long, dynamic, and highly differentiated granular textures, fulfilling its intended functionality and introducing an element of controlled randomness into the compositional process.

Subsequent to the algorithmic generation, the raw sound streams underwent meticulous manual refinement within a digital audio workstation (DAW). This phase involved selectively extracting and shaping the background layers to ensure their seamless integration with the foreground elements.

Orpheus of the Oracles

It may initially appear paradoxical that, over two decades ago, experimental music composers were already grappling with the consequences of an excessively technologized artistic practice. These composers recognized that an overreliance on technology could diminish spontaneity, stifle inspiration, and reduce the overall enjoyment inherent in the creative process.

In response to these challenges, several composers who possessed proficiency in software coding began to develop their own electronic music tools. These self-developed instruments were intentionally designed to introduce elements of surprise and unpredictability, thereby encouraging composers to venture beyond their established creative boundaries.

One notable example of this innovative approach is Eric Lyon's concept of "oracular synthesis" (Lyon 2002). Oracular synthesis represents a paradigm where the synthesis process is guided by algorithmic unpredictability, allowing the software to generate unexpected sonic outcomes that the composer can then interpret and integrate into their work. Lyon's oracular synthesis serves as a testament to the potential of indeterminate methodologies in fostering creative exploration and maintaining the dynamic essence of musical composition.

Furthermore, the development of such tools underscores the importance of identifying potential in the relationship between composers and their instruments. Even as technology automates labor-intensive tasks, the ability of these tools to resonate with the composer's personal artistic vision remains crucial. Oracular synthesis, despite the high level of randomness that it introduces in the workflow, allows composers to retain a deep connection to their work, ensuring that the resulting compositions are both innovative and authentically reflective of their creative identities:

> "Composers of digital music today have a bewildering variety of sound-processing tools and techniques at their disposal. At their best, these tools allow composers to hone a sound to perfection. However, they can also lead us into a routine which bypasses avenues of experimentation, simply because the known tools work so well and their sonic output is so attractive. An alternative strategy is oracular sound processing. An oracular sound processor creates a derived version of its input whose characteristics could not have been fully predicted, while affording the user little or no parametric control over the process..." (Lyon 2002)

Orpheus in a RAVE:
Timbre Transfer via Variable Autoencoders

RAVE (Realtime Audio Variational AutoEncoder) is a pioneering project developed by IRCAM in Paris that leverages variational autoencoders (VAEs) for real-time timbre transfer and synthesis. This innovative tool is designed to manipulate and transform audio signals by learning latent representations of sound, thereby enabling a wide array of creative applications such as morphing between different timbres, generating novel sounds, and more (Caillon et Esling 2021).

With RAVE, timbre transfer is achieved through a meticulous training process where the VAE is exposed to a diverse dataset of sounds. The encoder component compresses these sounds into a latent space, effectively capturing their essential features and underlying structures. During the timbre transfer process, an input sound is first encoded into this latent space. The decoder then reconstructs the sound, infusing it with the timbral characteristics of a designated target sound. This functionality is made possible because the latent space learned by the VAE encompasses the wide range of timbral variations present in the training data, enabling the model to seamlessly blend and morph these characteristics in real time.

By manipulating the latent representations within this space, users can transition smoothly between different timbres or create entirely new sound textures. This capability has been particularly employed to develop RAVE into a powerful voice transformation tool, allowing for significant modifications and enhancements in vocal timbre. Such transformations can range from subtle alterations that maintain the recognizability of the original voice to radical changes that render it almost unrecognizable, thereby expanding the creative possibilities for vocal manipulation in musical compositions.

The ability to parametrically describe the latent spaces involved in this variation process marks a significant shift from traditional compositional logic to a more organizational logic. In conventional composition, elements are typically chosen and arranged individually by the composer based on aesthetic or structural considerations. However, with RAVE, these elements can form the basis of a structured reconstruction process.

Here, the composer sets specific parameters and guidelines for automatic variation, allowing the tool to generate complex soundscapes that adhere to predefined criteria while introducing elements of variation and complexity that might not be immediately apparent through manual composition alone.

The Journey of Orpheus and Euridyce in the Neural Realm

Working with RAVE in both compositional and improvisational contexts has presented significant challenges. To explore its creative potential, we conducted extensive improvisation sessions utilizing live input and real-time control.

The setup for these improvisation sessions involved a soprano voice and a soprano saxophone feeding into the VST version of RAVE via live microphones, while an electronic music improviser controlled the eight latent parameters of the encoder through a MIDI controller. This configuration enabled dynamic interaction between performers and the algorithm.

The outputs of these sessions were recorded, carefully selected, curated, and edited by hand, with an emphasis on preserving the original sequences to capture the neural network's formal intelligence. Different pre-trained models developed by IRCAM and third parties, trained on nature soundscapes, orchestral instruments and voices were employed. The singer and saxophonist produced a vast palette of sound gestures while attentively listening to the blending of the input sound with RAVE's output, while the electronic improviser adjusted the parameters to understand their influence on the timbral transfer process.

Achieving effective interplay among the instruments, voices, electronic improviser, and the algorithm required numerous hours of work. This process challenged traditional ideas of parametric prediction and complete randomness, necessitating both technical adjustments and creative flexibility from the performers. There was a constant suggestion that establishing a meaningful link between the performers and the algorithm was both possible and necessary, although the underlying mechanisms remained partially obscure. This interaction highlighted the fact that the autoencoder responds to longer temporal scales of similitude rather than the instantaneous timbre structures of the models and live input. This finding challenges the traditional concept of similarity, encouraging performers to consider the temporal articulation of timbre rather than viewing sound as a fixed spectrum.

Overall, working with RAVE was a demanding experience that required the adaptation of both the human performers and the machine. This mutual adaptation was crucial in developing a coherent and effective collaborative process, demonstrating the complexities involved in integrating advanced machine learning tools into musical composition and improvisation. Despite these challenges, the experience proved highly rewarding, particularly given that all performers involved possessed extensive experience in traditional mixed music live electronic practices. This approach offers an important perspective for performers, facilitating the development of new competences that are both cognitive and aural, as well as enhancing their aesthetic and poetic sensibilities. By engaging with artificial creativity tools, performers can expand their skill sets and embrace innovative methods of musical expression, ultimately contributing to the evolution of contemporary compositional practices.

Conclusion

The Never-Ending Power of Orpheus

This methodological shift aligns with some of the conceptual frameworks theorized by Karlheinz Stockhausen in his 1954 essay on composition theory, which discussed the distinctions between composer invention and the utilization of pre-ordered material (Stockhausen 1954).

By employing artificial creativity tools and concepts, especially those based on neural networks, composers can effectively blend invention with organization, utilizing algorithmic processes to handle intricate sound manipulations while retaining overall control and intentionality in the compositional outcome. This convergence underscores the evolving relationship between technology and creativity in contemporary music, highlighting how advanced computational tools can augment the compositional process without undermining the artist's creative agency.

References

Barret, Natasha. Structuring processes in electroacoustic composition (Doctoral dissertation). London: City University, 1997.

Barthes, R. Fragments d'un discours amoureux. English, 1st American ed. New York: Hill and Wang, 1978, 1978.

Caillon, Antoine, and Philippe Esling. "RAVE: A variational autoencoder for fast and high-quality neural audio synthesis." *arXiv preprint arXiv:2111.05011*, 2021.

Cinelli, L. P., M. A. Marins, E. A. B. Da Silva, and S. L. Netto. "Variational autoencoder." In *In Variational Methods for Machine Learning with Applications to Deep Networks*, 111-149. Springer International Publishing, 2021.

Emmerson, Thomas Simons. *Analysis and the composition of electro-acoustic music*. London: The City University, 1982.

Esling, Philippe, and Ninon Devis. "Creativity in the era of artificial intelligence." *arXiv preprint arXiv:2008.05959*, 2020.

Kingma, Diederik P. Auto-encoding variational bayes. *arXiv preprint arXiv:1312.6114*, 2013.

Landy, Leigh. "The "something to hold on to factor" in timbral composition." In *Timbre Composition in Electroacoustic Music*, 49-60. Routledge, 2019.

Lyon, E., Mathews, M., McCartney, J., Zicarelli, D., Vercoe, B., Loy, G., & Puckette, M. "Dartmouth symposium on the future of computer music software: A panel discussion." *Computer Music Journal*, 2002: 26(4), 13-30.

Malt, M. Some Considerations on Brian Ferneyhough's Musical Language–Part I. Vol. 2, in *The OM composer's book 2,* by Carlos, Gérard Assayag, and Jean Bresson Agon. Editions Delatour France/Ircam-Centre Pompidou, 2006.

Manaris, Bill & Roos, Patrick & Machado, Penousal & Krehbiel, Dwight & Pellicoro, Luca & Romero, Juan. "A Corpus-Based Hybrid Approach to Music Analysis and Composition." In *Proceedings of the National Conference on Artificial Intelligence.* 2007. 839-845.

Merleau-Ponty, M. *Phénoménologie de la Perception.* Éditions Gallimard, 1945.

Moruzzi, C. "Measuring creativity: an account of natural and artificial creativity." *European Journal for Philosophy of Science*, 2021: 11(1), 1.

Ratoci, A. "Annotation automatique et (re) composition: poétique et technique d'un flux de travaux par base de données." In *Journées d'Informatique Musicale*, JIM 2020, 2020.

Ratoci, A. "Rima Flow: Oral tradition and composition." In *OM Composer's Book III*, by Jean, Carlos Agón, and Gérard Assayag, eds Bresson, 321-340. Paris: Ircam, Centre Pompidou, 2016.

Robert, A. "La fabrication d'œuvres de musique contemporaine: Une enquête auprès de compositeurs en formation." *Sociétés contemporaines*, no. 119(2) (2021): 115-141.

Runco, M. "AI can only produce artificial creativity." *Journal of Creativity* Volume 33, no. Issue 3 (2023).

Schwarz, D., Britton, S., Cahen, R., & Goepfer, T. "Musical applications of real-time corpus-based concatenative synthesis." In *International Computer Music Conference* (ICMC) . 2007. 47-50.

Stockhausen, K. "Situation actuelle du métier de compositeur." In: *Domaine musicale,* 1954: S. 126-141; s. hz. Texte I, S. 45-61.

Takale, D. G., P. N. Mahalle, and B. Sule. "Generative AI Models: A Comparative Analysis." *Journal of Computer Science Engineering and Software Testing*, 2024: 10(1), 32-38.

Wishart, Trevor. *"Audible design."* York: Orpheus the Pantomime, 1994.

Chapter 5

I-Artist: New Ways to Compose

Alessandro Camatta[*]
and Luca Ferliga[†]
Course of Audio Production, SAE Institute Milan, Milan, Italy

Abstract

The project "I-Artist: New Ways to Compose" is based on the premise that artificial intelligence can stimulate the creative process by complementing the abilities and tools of those who use it. The project team committed to creating an extended musical piece (approximately 6 minutes long) which incorporated AI contributions at every stage of the process (recording, composition, sampling, mixing and mastering). In the recording phase, timbre morphing software allowed the transformation of guitar recordings into other instruments such as woodwinds, thus overcoming traditional time and budget constraints. Regarding composition, artificial intelligence played a role in suggesting unique harmonic combinations and intriguing melodies, thereby opening new creative possibilities. Moving forward, sound synthesis tools enabled the generation of audio clips based on textual prompts, allowing to create specific sound textures without sifting through dozens of sound packs. Finally, in the mixing and mastering stages, softwares packages capable of providing processing parameters by analyzing the input audio tracks supplied auxiliary tools to the Mix Engineer. Therefore, artificial intelligence played a central role in the project by proposing and generating a series of inputs. However, the human element remained indispensable, as it curated the generated content and fused it into a cohesive whole with the goal of achieving the best of both worlds. From

---

[*] Corresponding Author's Email: 17-13821@saeinstitute.edu
[†] Corresponding Author's Email: 17-13655@saeinstitute.edu

In: Computational Arts and Creative Products
Editor: Alessandra Micalizzi
ISBN: 979-8-89530-426-6
© 2025 Nova Science Publishers, Inc.

a stylistic perspective, the project attempted to conciliate two seemingly distant worlds: Popular and Ambient Music. The former was chosen for its ability to appeal to human emotions by recalling familiar sounds and melodic or rhythmic cells, while the latter provided a more intellectual angle by integrating unconventional compositional logics, such as sampling non-musical sounds and structures unbound by the concept of a song. Thus, this is a very ambitious project that aims to impact and destabilize its audience while simultaneously rebuilding trust in the logic of the creative process, bending the unstoppable power of artificial intelligence to the judgment of human emotion. The research questions that guided the production of the project were fundamentally two: is it possible today to integrate tools that utilize artificial intelligence in musical production? In which practices is the standard qualitatively high, and in which areas is there still a long way to go before satisfactory results are achieved?

Keywords: ambient music, popular music, artificial intelligence

Introduction

In recent years, artificial intelligence (AI) has burst into various sectors revolutionizing established practices and processes. The world of music is no exception. In this field, AI not only expands the possibilities of creation but also helps break down barriers, making music more accessible and personalized. For instance, Spotify recently introduced a feature that creates playlists from simple phrases (Spotify, 2024).

This feature can be extremely useful not just for personal listening but also in various professional settings like offices and retail stores. Other applications include song search - Cyanite has developed a web app capable of automatically tagging its catalog, allowing searches based on features like mood and movement (Cyanite, n.d.) - and automatic generation of sounds for films, advertisements and video games (Thom, 2024). Narrowing the focus to music production, there are now innovative systems - like Suno (Suno, n.d.) or AIVA (AIVA, n.d.) - capable of composing songs independently, which could suggest a type of replacement for human composers. However, many artists view AI not as a substitute, but as a creative partner. Musicians can input their compositions into AI systems, allowing artificial intelligence to suggest new directions (Jamahook, n.d.). AI can serve as an endless source of inspiration. By analyzing inputs, AI can identify patterns and combinations that humans might overlook (Magenta, n.d.), helping musicians to break through creative blocks and explore new genres or styles. AI also opens up new frontiers in sound design, allowing musicians to experiment with sounds previously unimaginable.

Neural networks can generate entirely new timbres and textures, expanding the sonic palette available to artists (Magenta, n.d.). This leads to the creation of unique and innovative musical pieces that challenge conventional norms and push artistic boundaries. Briefly, AI offers new opportunities for musical creation, not replacing the human touch but enriching it and expanding creative possibilities. With these premises, the future of music promises to be more diverse, innovative and emotionally resonant. This project was created with the intention of exploring this synergy between human and machine in the compositional process. This includes melody generation, sound processing and mixing and mastering phases. It was decided to work on two distinct musical genres with the aim of blending them together: Pop and Ambient. Pop music, with its catchy melodies and rhythms, provided a traditional context in which to apply AI techniques, ensuring that the result was accessible and ear-catching. The melodic structures of Pop are often simple yet effective, built around rhythmic cells that remain ingrained in the listener's memory.

The Pop genre was chosen not only for its popularity and immediacy but also for its ability to evoke human emotions through recognizable, memorable sounds. Touching the emotional chords of the audience, recalling memories and associations tied to listening to specific genres, and emotionally connecting with the listener: Pop inherently possesses these evocative qualities. This factor was really important for the project and allowed us to combine the technical innovation of AI with the emotional impact of popular music. On the other hand, Ambient Music, with its generative and experimental nature, lends itself particularly well to the use of generative AI techniques. Thanks to unconventional compositional logics – such as sampling non-musical sounds, which permitted the exploration of new sound textures and environments – and structures detached from the concept of a song – more expansive and freer from the need to maintain focused attention – the project would be more stimulating from a creative and experimental standpoint.

Creative Process

The pre-production stage involved defining the concept and genre and selecting the tools and techniques to employ. In the initial meetings, there was extensive discussion on how artificial intelligence could significantly contribute to the creative process, from generating initial ideas to finalizing the product. Subsequently, the focus shifted to finding the appropriate tools to carry out the identified tasks for the AI. The composition stage was divided into several sub-phases, listed chronologically as follows:

- *Composition of the main pad*: created using the AI tool Chord Progression in FL Studio 24 (Beta), this task defined the harmonic foundation of the production;
- *Melody generation*: achieved with the AI tool Google Magenta Studio 2.0, this task enriched the harmonic base with relaxed yet intriguing melodies realized with a tool capable of MIDI scores generation. From this point onwards, the production shifted to Live 12, equipped with MIDI editing features;
- *Composition of bass lines*: created without the aid of AI, this task covered the low octave and defined the rhythmic structure to be followed by the percussion section;
- *Recording of secondary melodies with contrapuntal roles*: also completed without AI assistance, this task created call-and-response elements with the main melody, adding engagement to the composition;
- *Composition of rhythmic cells*: executed without AI support, this task added marked and distinguishable rhythms typical of Pop Music;
- *Arrangement of environmental sound samples*: completed without AI assistance using the Session View in Live 12, which employs algorithmic logic to randomize the clips playback within the track. This task added random elements typical of Ambient Music.

Wherever possible, the decision was made to utilize AI, while other tasks were carried out personally by the team. After each AI intervention, the material was refined to ensure better integration into the project. For instance, some notes of the chords were inverted or duplicated in higher octaves, while the melody was modified when it did not adhere to the desired rhythm. The arrangement phase, however, was conducted concurrently with the production of the elements and thus did not require additional time. Given the hybrid nature of the piece, an extended intro was created that leads into a sort of verse, with a climax (comparable to a chorus) occurring upon the introduction of all rhythmic elements. Finally, the production was concluded with an outro. To avoid a too-obvious perception of transitions between sections, 12-bar loops were used instead of the canonical 8 (the duration of each section, however, is quite long as the work was done at 24 BPM). All parts were composed with reference genres in mind to achieve a hybrid composition even before considering the sounds. The production phase was also divided into several sub-phases, some of which coincided with those of the composition. Given the digital workflow, the two phases tended to overlap since sound production is necessarily accompanied by its composition and arrangement:

- *Production of the main pad (overlapping through layering of multiple sound pads):* created without AI assistance using stock sounds from Logic Pro 11. This task initially established the sound to pursue throughout the production. The other elements were produced to effectively complement the sounds of the main pad;
- *Production of the melody sound:* created without AI assistance using the digital synth xFer Serum. The chosen sound was a Pluck, later affected by various effects such as reverbs and random pitch modulations;
- *Production of the bass line sounds*: created without AI assistance utilizing various available synths and samples, particularly Operator for the first bass - a Live 12 stock synthesizer equipped with a multi-oscillator engine -, Moog Minimoog for the second bass - a digital synth produced by Universal emulating the well-known Moog Minimoog Model D, known for its iconic sound -, and an 808 sample for the third bass, audible in the Outro - a typically more percussive bass sound derived from the Roland TR-808 drum machine, widely adopted in many genres since the 1980s (e.g., Dance or Hip-Hop). This task aimed to achieve sounds from both reference genres even in the lower part of the spectrum (Ambient for the first bass and Pop for the second and third);
- *Timbre morphing of the secondary melody*: achieved with the Tuba model from the AI tool Magenta DDSP Effect, this task transformed the sound of a DI guitar into a timbre similar to a flute, adding an element that would otherwise not have been available;

- *Warping of rhythmic samples*: created without AI, this task produced typically Pop sounds for the percussion section. Warping and quantization allowed the samples to be stretched without altering their pitch and timing them to adhere to the desired rhythm;
- *Generation of ambient sound samples*: created using the AI tool Text to Sample, which generates audio samples from textual prompts, this task added an ambient sound texture typical of Ambient Music. Again, the samples were stretched and quantized as desired.

As before, wherever possible, the decision was made to utilize artificial intelligence, while other tasks were carried out personally by the team. After each AI intervention, the material was refined to ensure better integration into the project. For instance, the timbre morphing was realized starting from a recording played an octave higher than the typical range of a tuba to obtain a higher sound, while the ambient sound samples were stretched and processed (thus not used as they were originally generated). All incorporated sounds were inspired by the reference genres to achieve a result with hybrid and coherent sound qualities. The mixing process involved the use of SmartComp and SmartEQ to enhance the quality of the sound and reach an industry standard. Other processors were used (such as multiband compressors, bus compressors, various modulation effects etc.) which will not be detailed to avoid excessive technicalities. During mastering, iZotope Ozone 10 Mastering Assistant provided a starting point for the mastering chain, which was then modified to better suit the musical style adopted in the production. The integration of a dynamic resonance suppressor and analog simulations completed the process, ensuring a polished and professional final sound.

Production and Recording

Various DAWs (Digital Audio Workstations) were used for the project, each chosen for its unique characteristics. The first one was FL Studio. Developed by Image-Line (Image-Line, n.d.), it is one of the most popular and well-regarded DAWs. It was chosen for this project because of its Chord Progression tool, a powerful and versatile instrument designed to facilitate the creation of chord sequences, a fundamental element in musical composition. Accessible via Piano Roll, it features an intuitive interface that allows quick selection among various types of chords and progressions, as well as setting musical parameters (number of beats or bar length, preset progressions or scales, rhythms, use of diatonic notes), suggestions on the desired mood (conventional rather than adventurous, safe rather than unusual, genre, use of alterations) and instructions for the AI (how much to consider the first chord of the progression while generating the last one, how much to consider the position of the chord within the metric, whether to repeat the same chord multiple times, number of notes per chord, etc.). Once generated, the progression is transferred to the Piano Roll and can be manually edited by the user to create inversions, transpose to other tonalities, customize dynamics or use other tools like Arpeggiator or Strumming. The generated progression - B min7, A min9, D7+ - was played at a very slow tempo (24 BPM), ideal for an ambient instrumental. The first two chords served as the foundation, while the last one appeared in the final section. The main advantages in the utilization of FL Studio were:

- *Ease of Use*: its intuitive interface makes the tool accessible even to beginners;
- *Creativity and Flexibility*: it allows exploration of a wide range of sounds and harmonies;
- *Efficiency:* it speeds up the composition process enabling a quick creation of chord progressions;
- *Integration*: it seamlessly integrates with FL Studio's workflow, allowing easy manipulation and customization of progressions.

The Chord Progression tool proved to be an asset for composers and music producers due to its ease of use and creative power. With its advanced features and ability to customize every aspect of the chords, it enables the creation of musically rich harmonic progressions adaptable to any musical genre. The second DAW used was Logic Pro 11, developed by Apple, Inc. (Apple, n.d.). It is one of the most appreciated DAWs among MacOS users, and in the context of this project it was used to create the sound layers of the Pad, essential for providing the song's sonic foundation. It was specifically chosen for its high-quality Lo-Fi timbre sounds organized by groups of virtual instruments (a feature found to be very useful for performing an initial mix of the various layers of the pad). The main advantages in the utilization of Logic Pro 11 were:

- *Sounds far from digital cleanliness*: the timbre of the stock sounds is multifaceted and composed with several layers dedicated to background noises, distortion, rhythmic details, modulations;
- *Functional organization of sound layers*: each sound consists of many grouped virtual instruments. Each of these is loaded with its opening and can be modified individually, thus offering extensive customization possibilities.

In conclusion, Logic Pro 11 virtual instruments offer numerous advantages for music production. The ability to generate sounds that avoid typical digital cleanliness thanks to complex and layered timbres brings the sounds closer to the traits of the analog domain. Moreover, the organization of sound layers allows grouping various virtual instruments - each assigned to a different mixer track - into a single sound, offering a high degree of customization and creative flexibility. These elements make Logic Pro 11 an excellent choice for the production of Ambient music tracks. The third DAW used was Ableton Live 12. Developed by Ableton (Ableton, n.d.), it is among the favorite DAWs of DJs and performers particularly because it is designed with two parallel windows, one for studio composition and the other for live performance execution. It is very versatile and allows for different workflows. After creating the main foundation of the track, Live 12 was used for its powerful sample manipulation capabilities - particularly stretching and quantization for the rhythmic loops - and the Session View screen, which integrates algorithmic logics to randomly play audio clips loaded within the same track. Having little control over some elements of the composition, as Brian Eno (Eno, 1996) noted describing his idea of generative music, is a vital aspect for an Ambient Music track, as it introduces a random element that allows distancing from the human contribution and provides a sense of movement over time, despite the elements remaining the same for several minutes. The clips used were generated with specific tools and processed with effects - including pitch modulations, ambient effects, flangers and compressors - to achieve a uniform sound texture. Other elements produced on Live 12 included bass and melodic lines, which were then arranged in the Arrangement View and mixed with other elements. The main advantages in the utilization of Ableton Live 12 were:

- Dual interface: the coexistence of SessionView and Arrangement View allows for a production that integrates both random and time-defined elements;
- Warping and Time Stretching: the powerful warping engine enables precise temporal and tonal manipulations, allowing samples to be slowed down multiple times without significant quality loss.

In summary, Live 12 stands out for its versatility and power thanks to its dual interface. This coexistence offers producers the freedom to combine random and predefined elements, facilitating both improvised composition and the construction of complex musical structures. Additionally, Live 12 powerful warping and time-stretching engine allows for precise temporal and tonal manipulations, ensuring high audio quality even after numerous modifications. These features make Live 12 an indispensable tool for musicians and producers seeking flexibility, creativity, and absolute control over their music production process. Furthermore, various AI-based tools and plugins were integrated at different stages of the project. Google Magenta Studio 2.0 represents a significant innovation in AI-assisted musical composition. This tool not only facilitates the generation of MIDI data through advanced machine learning models but also offers a wide range of functionalities to manipulate and customize musical compositions. For this project, Studio 2.0 was used to create the main melody starting from an existing MIDI file (the chord progression). Using parameters like the Temperature, it was possible to adjust the degree of originality and complexity of the melody generated by the machine learning model. Increasing it, the tool was encouraged to explore bolder and more unexpected solutions, while decreasing it, the tool maintained closer coherence with the theme and style of the track (Magenta, n.d.). Magenta Studio's ability to provide immediate feedback and continuously generate new ideas allowed for the efficient exploration of multiple melodic variants. After finding a version of the melody that reflected the project's artistic vision, the result was integrated into the track and finally refined and adapted to the other instrumental parts. TensorFlow Magenta DDSP (Differentiable Digital Signal Processing) Effect is a cutting-edge tool that applies deep learning to digital signal processing, allowing transformation and manipulation of instrument timbres in entirely new ways. Among its main features, the standout is Timbre Transfer, which enables the transformation of an instrument's timbre into another. For instance, it is possible to take the sound of a guitar and make it sound like a violin or a trumpet.

This ability to alter timbres opens up various creative possibilities, offering musicians the freedom to explore sounds they could otherwise not integrate into their compositions (Magenta, 2022). Within this project, DDSP Effect was used to morph the timbre of a DI guitar using the "tuba" model, available among the presets. The guitar was played at a higher register than the typical range of a tuba, resulting in a timbre similar to a flute. Fully leveraging the creative potential offered by the Magenta DDSP Effect demonstrated how AI integration can lead to surprising and innovative musical results by transforming the original sound into something entirely new. This technique added an element of uniqueness and experimentation to the composition, introducing a new prospect to the creative process and highlighting how AI integration can enrich music with astonishing results. Text to Sample is an innovative tool that leverages generative artificial intelligence to convert textual prompts or audio files into audio samples.

For instance, one can input a prompt like "nighttime city atmosphere" and receive an audio sample that reflects this description. Additionally, it offers the ability to extend and further develop the audio samples provided by the user. It uses generative AI to analyze and understand the initial sample and generate continuations that aim to maintain the character and style of the original file (Samplab, n.d.). This resource is particularly useful to accelerate the creative process providing a solid foundation upon which users can build musical ideas. In this project, Text to Sample was employed to create distinctive audio samples based on specific textual descriptions. The generated results, unfortunately, did not have the best audio quality, so they were selected and processed to be enriched and achieve a uniform and intriguing sound texture. After the initial generation, each sample was carefully processed through warping, stretching and effects that modulated pitch and timbre to achieve the desired sonic atmosphere, ensuring that every sound element integrated seamlessly into the context of the piece. But the role of this tool has remained significant: it has not only expanded creative possibilities but also enriched the musical production with unique and customized sounds, helping to define the sonic identity of the composition.

Mixing and Mastering

For mixing and mastering, a range of advanced tools that incorporate AI were used to enhance the process. Starting with the mixing, the main tools were SmartComp and SmartEQ by Sonible, two advanced audio processing tools based on AI and designed to enhance sound quality during the mixing process. These software tools operate by analyzing the incoming audio and providing detailed suggestions for compression and equalization, respectively. SmartComp is a compressor that uses machine learning algorithms to analyze the audio signal and propose optimal compression settings. This process aims to maintain transparent and musical compression, adapting to the specific characteristics of the sound while preserving the natural dynamics of the music. Instead, SmartEQ is an equalizer that examines the frequency content of the audio. Through advanced analysis, it suggests equalization curves to correct frequency issues and improve the clarity and definition of the final mix. SmartEQ is particularly effective in balancing the different sound components of a track and ensuring that each element is well-positioned within the overall soundscape. During the mixing process of the piece, the combined use of SmartComp and SmartEQ reliably suggested the necessary interventions. Not only did they optimize the sound automatically and accurately, but they also allowed for greater focus on the creative aspects of mixing. Thanks to their analytical and suggestive capabilities, the production sound was refined and perfected, achieving results that fully reflect the artistic vision.

Then, iZotope Ozone 10 was employed for the mastering stage. This advanced audio mastering suite incorporates various AI-based features to optimize the music post-production process, including the Mastering Assistant, which analyzes the final mix of a track and suggests a complete mastering chain. This chain includes crucial steps such as equalization, compression, stereo imaging adjustments and limiting. The AI of the Mastering Assistant dynamically adapts the settings of these processes to the specific sonic characteristics of the track, providing an optimal starting point for the final refinement of the piece. In addition to the Mastering Assistant, iZotope Ozone 10 offers advanced tools like Match EQ, which allows for comparing and adapting the frequency profile of the track to a desired reference, ensuring optimal frequency balance. The Dynamic EQ and Imager tools provide detailed control over the dynamics and spatiality of the sound, contributing to a professional and well-balanced final mix. Finally, the Maximizer uses limiting algorithms to increase the perceived volume of the track.

The combined use of these features allows a final mastering result to be achieved that reflects the track genre, enhancing the overall quality of the music production and ensuring a final sound that meets the aesthetic and technical needs of the piece in question. Within the production, characterized by an Ambient nature, the initial suggestions provided by the Mastering Assistant were used as a baseline. However, significant modifications were necessary to tailor them to the specific sound context of the piece, which was initially misinterpreted by the Mastering Assistant due to the hybrid nature of the composition. Some corrections included removing stereo image reductions and dynamic boosts in the high end of the spectrum and replacing the limiter with a Fabfilter Pro-L2. As cited before, the mastering process also included the integration of corrective plug-ins, such as the dynamic resonance suppressor Soothe 2 and analog simulations like Hitsville EQ and SSL Fusion Transformer, placed before Ozone 10 to further refine the sound and address specific sonic characteristics of the track.

Conclusion

This project has demonstrated how artificial intelligence can be a powerful ally in music creation, expanding creative possibilities and enhancing the efficiency of the production process. The chords generated with the Chord Progression tools, the melodies produced by Magenta Studio 2.0 and the timbres transformed by Magenta DDSP Effect added a new dimension to our piece, while the samples generated by Text to Sample accelerated the search process. Additionally, the AI-based mixing and mastering tools contributed to achieve a professional sound. However, there are still challenges to be overcome: the Chord Progression tool, for example, did not seem to genuinely understand the psychoacoustic effect of each chord it generates, nor the effect of its combination with another chord, requiring the user to have enough musical theory knowledge to correct its shortcomings with inversions, augmentations or diminutions, etc. The Google Magenta Studio 2.0 melody generator also did not appear capable of coherently relating to the other scores in the project. Even when provided with MIDI scores as a starting point, it failed to produce emotionally engaging melodies. The ambient sound samples generated by Text to Sample adhered to the text prompt regarding timbral quality, but had envelopes not found in either natural or artificial sounds, resulting in a synthesized sound that bears little resemblance to sounds hearable in real contexts.

Additionally, the generation process still takes a considerable amount of time, allowing for savings in the mere search for samples, but requiring significant effort in a later phase of the project, where samples need to be processed or edited for an effective integration. The mixing tools SmartComp and SmartEQ proved to be very useful, but their extensive use revealed a noticeable reliance on models: while sound analysis appeared effective in identifying some macro-interventions based on the type of sound (e.g., percussion versus string instruments), its ability to understand the microscopic characteristics that differentiate a guitar intended for a rock piece versus a folk piece seemed poor. The suggested interventions would be the same, simply because, in its view, it is just a guitar. Lastly, the iZotope Ozone 10 Mastering Assistant analysis of the genre of the track often led to incorrect interpretations. Consequently, suggested interventions could be inaccurate due to a fundamental misunderstanding (e.g., equalization that does not respect the typical frequency curve of the actual genre of the composition, excessive limiting to achieve loudness levels that are too high for the piece being mastered etc.).

Sometimes the identified genre may not even be present in the available list, forcing the user to compromise and select the most similar one. Throughout the project, many challenges were faced, including ensuring that the materials produced with the AI tools met the qualitative and artistic standards, as well as the need to manually modify the mixing and mastering tools automatic suggestions. These experiences highlighted the importance of a balanced approach, where AI supports but does not replace human judgment and creativity. In the future, it is anticipated that AI tools will be refined and improved, leading to continued exploration of this fascinating intersection between technology and art. The success of "I-Artist: New Ways to Compose" has inspired further exploration of AI in music: the aim will be to experiment new techniques and integrate AI into the production process, seeking new ways to push the boundaries of musical creativity and express the artistic vision of musicians and producers. The project has demonstrated how AI can transform the creative process in music by offering new opportunities to explore innovative sounds and compositions. AI can become a valuable collaborator, capable of expanding creative possibilities and enhancing the overall quality of the final product. It is hoped that its role will remain supportive and won't overshadow the human contribution, which is essential in the current state of the art. The project team hopes that this chapter has provided a detailed and inspiring overview of the work accomplished, highlighting both the potentiality and the challenges that still need to be addressed in integrating AI into the world of music. As we can see, the model introduces AI, connected with individual and domains. In fact, the integration of Artificial Intelligence, individuals or groups develop rule-based algorithms that enable computational modeling, pattern recognition, and predictive capabilities. Rather than receiving direct inputs from the environment, the AI is programmed to adapt to the information it encounters within the domain, thereby expanding and modifying the potential for new permutations (Atkinson, Barker 2023).

However, if we recall the definition of art and creativity proposed in the first section, we can clearly see that this model underestimates the role of the public, that is the importance of being recognized, culturally and socially, as a product of art.

Several studies (among others Latikka et al. 2023) highlight how the users are less prepared to identify what is produced by AI, even if remains some forms of bias. More specifically, at the beginning of the discussion about Artificial Creativity, if solicited, the public pointed out the low quality of AI-generated productions, even if, after blind tests it appears more as a prejudice than real evidence (Micalizzi, 2024). Over the last years, the level of awareness has risen, and the public is more and more open to appreciate the quality of AI's creative outputs, accepting the difficulties of distinguishing what is created by AI and what is not. Several studies have demonstrated a growing acceptance of artificially created or co-created products (Hong, 2021). For instance, research (Elgammal et al. 2017) showed that artificial intelligence can be employed to produce automated artworks that consumers are unable to distinguish from human-created ones. Elgammal and collaborators (2017) further discovered that machine-generated products were often preferred over human-made ones, receiving higher scores on attributes such as novelty, complexity, intentionality, and inspiration. Similarly, Hadjeres, Pachet, and Nielsen (2017) used a generative model called DeepBach to create new compositions based on the works of Johann Sebastian Bach. In tests, nearly half of the participants categorized the AI-generated music as "original." However, the results indicated that as musical expertise increased, fewer participants (40%) believed the machine-generated music was composed by Bach.

These findings were later corroborated by experimental studies, including those by Hong and Curran (2019) and Tigre Moura and collaborators (2021), which revealed that while respondents held somewhat negative views of AI being used for music composition, knowing AI was involved had minimal impact on their perception of the resulting compositions.

What we would like to stress with a quick carousel of several empirical research is that in the process of recognition of AI-generated products as forms of creativity and expression of art, there are some variables that intervene: the level of awareness or opacity of the use of these technologies in the art production; the biases connected with the old-fashion imagery about an AI that is rational, unemotional and unable to reproduce typical human skills (confirmed by several experiments); the weight of the ethical issues especially connected to the authorship and the value of the artistic production.

As can be imagined, each of the points ranked above represents a crucial point in the public debate about the complex topic of arts, artificial intelligence and socio-cultural implications. In these pages, we aim to offer a possible interpretation of the phenomenon that, in some ways, disconnects the concept of art from the product in the strict sense, and in a dialogical and cultural perspective, stressing the role of the experience.

If we emphasize the experience as the pivotal moment of "having art," art can be considered as a verb, as suggested by Ketie Compton (2022). The author abandons the old categories to define an artwork as such – the author, the materiality, the cultural value etc. – to put the attention on the experience, recontextualizing the concept of art within Bauman's metaphor of postmodernity. In this way, art also becomes liquid, in contrast to the "solid" and monolithic view of the past.

Liquid art (ivi) can be defined as a space of potential artistic artifacts, navigated through the act of surfing and filtering, and experienced as streams or overwhelming waves, most commonly in an online environment. It refers to the phenomenon of encountering mass-produced artifacts, such as AI-generated imagery, in a context where their sheer abundance transforms the act of 'surfing' through this media into the experience of art itself (Smith, Cook 2023). The centrality of experience in creating (liquid) art redefines the role of AI, which becomes one of the elements at play in the dialogical process between artist, publics, culture, and artifact.

Even from this perspective, the ethical question regarding the use of sources and referentiality remains open, as well as the impact on public imagination and tastes. This is particularly relevant in relation to a quantitatively infinite production that is still limited in variety and primarily focused on generating approval (audience interests) rather than innovating or conveying a message (author's intentions).

We can only hope for a more open and trusting attitude that can lead towards experimentation, while adhering to ethically sound objectives.

Maybe it is possible to imagine e new way to observe and frame art and creativity in their relationship with technologies. Maybe, it is possible to overcome the topic of authorship if we use the perspective proposed by D'Isa (2024), the author who opens this publication. Provocatively, D'Isa asks an important question: what is the true innovation brought by AI in its connection with the art world really? D'Isa argues that, once again, we should see the artwork as the result of multiple factors, in which we traditionally isolate the human as the author. He suggests that "the shock caused by innovation has momentarily disrupted an interpretive habit, reminding us that it is not we who create, but the world." (ivi, p. 145).

References

Ableton. *Find yourself again and again in Ableton Live.* Ableton [online]. n.d. [Accessed July 12, 2024]. Available at: https://www.ableton.com/en/.
AIVA. *AIVA - Your personal AI music generation assistant.* AIVA [online]. n.d. [Accessed July 24, 2024]. Available at: https://www.aiva.ai/.
Apple. *Logic Pro Powerful. Creative. Smarter Than Ever.* Apple [online]. n.d. [Accessed July 12, 2024]. Available at: https://www.apple.com/it/logic-pro/.
Cyanite. For those who shape tomorrow's music industry. Cyanite [online]. n.d. [Accessed July 24, 2024]. Available at: https://cyanite.ai/.
Eno, B. *Generative Music* [speech]. Imagination Conference, San Francisco. 8 June. In Motion Magazine [online]. 1996. [Accessed July 12, 2024]. Available at: https://inmotionmagazine.com/eno1.html.
Image-Line. *Introducing FL Studio 24.* Image-Line [online]. n.d. [Accessed July 12, 2024]. Available at: https://www.image-line.com/.
Jamahook. *The world's only AI Sound Matching.* Jamahook [online]. n.d. [Accessed July 24, 2024]. Available at: https://jamahook.com/.
Magenta. *DDSP-VST: Neural Audio Synthesis for All.* Magenta [online]. 2022. [Accessed 12 July 2024]. Available at: https://magenta.tensorflow.org/ddsp-vst-blog.
Magenta. *Magenta Studio.* Magenta [online]. n.d. [Accessed 12 July 2024]. Available at: https://magenta.tensorflow.org/studio/.
Magenta. *Make Music and Art Using Machine Learning.* Magenta [online]. n.d. [Accessed July 24, 2024]. Available at: https://magenta.tensorflow.org/.
Magenta (2017). *NSynth: Neural Audio Synthesis.* 6 April. Magenta [online]. 2017. [Accessed July 24, 2024]. Available at: https://magenta.tensorflow.org/nsynth.
Samplab. *TextToSample | Samplab.* Samplab [online]. n.d. [Accessed 12 July 2024]. Available at: https://samplab.com/text-to-sample.
Spotify (2024). *Spotify Premium Users Can Now Turn Any Idea Into a Personalized Playlist With AI Playlist in Beta.* 24 April. Spotify [online]. 2024. [Accessed July 24, 2024]. Available at: https://newsroom.spotify.com/2024-04-07/spotify-premium-users-can-now-turn-any-idea-into-a-personalized-playlist-with-ai-playlist-in-beta/.
Suno. *Make a song about anything.* Suno [online]. n.d. [Accessed July 24, 2024]. Available at: https://suno.com/.
Thom, R. *Sound Design and AI.* 30 April. Sound Ideas [online]. 2024. [Accessed July 24, 2024]. Available at: https://www.sound-ideas.com/blog/Sound-Design-and-AI.

Chapter 6

Doomed to Fantasize?
Exploring the Implications of Critical Posthumanism for Creative Practices

Elisa Poli[*], PhD
NABA, Nuova Accademia di Belle Arti, Milan, Italy

Abstract

This paper analyzes the discourse concerning AI through narrative works understood both as plot and moving image, read as a phenomenological process and as a repository of philosophical theories. Considering classical parameters such as the subjects, the objects and the places of trans and posthuman iconography, examples related to science fiction in literature and screenwriting will be illustrated. The inquiry engages with instances from various books, films and TV series, best-known and celebrated science fiction masterpieces but, also, classical and philosophical texts, to understand how they encapsulates fulfilled premonitions and unresolved questions about the whirlwind technological growth. The discourse will focus on several themes that seek to overcome the hype of AI through the unravelling of the physical places of immateriality and characters of mediality (Black Mirror and Upload) but, especially, through a prescient and foundational book. "Emigrate or degenerate! The choice is yours!" is a quote, part of a government tag line, in Philip Dick's science fiction book, Do Androids Dream of Electric Sheep? The story is set in a post-apocalyptic San Francisco, where Earth's life has been greatly damaged by a nuclear global war, leaving most animal species endangered or extinct. The main

---

[*] Corresponding Author's Email: elisa.poli@naba.edu

In: Computational Arts and Creative Products
Editor: Alessandra Micalizzi
ISBN: 979-8-89530-426-6
© 2025 Nova Science Publishers, Inc.

plot follows Rick Deckard, a bounty hunter who is tasked with "retiring" (i.e., killing) six escaped Nexus-6 model androids. The hybridization of those androids allows them to be humans on the surface – skin - and robots in the inner parts. The distribution between human parts - tissues, organs, bones - and robotic parts - mechanical structure, actuators, sensors, control system - is not entirely specified in the book, and it is precisely this sophisticated and complex mixture that makes the Nexus powerful and touching hybrids, not only physically but, above all, emotionally and psychically. Is it the machines who have finally and permanently humanized themselves or, rather, is it the humans who have transferred into robotic and technological mechanization their hope for future and eternal life (Giedion, 1948)?

Keywords: artificial creativity, creative practices, visual art

Narrative and Iconography in Posthumanism

We shall therefore open with the question: what happens when mechanization meets an organic substance? And shall close by inquiry into the attitude of our culture toward our organism. x
Sigfried Giedion, Mechanization Takes Command

This paper analyses the discourse concerning posthumanism through narrative work (both plot and moving images), reading it as both a phenomenological process and a repository of philosophical theories. Considering classical parameters that include the subjects, objects and places of trans- and posthuman iconography, it examines examples related to the design, economic and social spheres. Where the paper uses the term "posthuman", it does so in reference to *critical* posthumanism: "a reinvention of some humanist values and methodologies which, in the face of a fundamental transformation provoked by digitalization and the advent of ubiquitous computing and social media, appear to have become obsolete, or to be in urgent need of revision" (Herbrechter, *European Posthumanism*). The paper examines examples from various creative disciplines, focusing primarily on a well-known and celebrated masterpiece of science fiction in order to understand its use of unresolved questions and the fulfilment of premonitions.

"Emigrate or degenerate! The choice is yours!" This line forms part of a government slogan in Philip K. Dick's science-fiction novel *Do Androids*

Dream of Electric Sheep? (1968). The story is set in a post-apocalyptic San Francisco when Earth's life has been greatly damaged by a global nuclear war, leaving most animal species endangered or extinct. The main plot follows Rick Deckard, a bounty hunter who is tasked with "retiring" (i.e., killing) six escaped androids. The Nexus-6 models' hybridization allows them to be humans on the surface, with organic skin, and robots on the inside. The distribution of parts between human ones – tissues, organs, bones – and robotic – mechanical structure, actuators, sensors, control system – is not entirely specified in the book, and it is precisely this sophisticated and complex mixture that makes the Nexus-6 powerful and evocative hybrids, not only physically but, above all, emotionally and psychologically. Have machines finally and permanently humanized themselves or, instead, have humans transferred their hopes for the future and eternal life into robotic and technological mechanization (Giedion)?

The text "Emigrate or degenerate" comes, in the novel, from an advertisement encouraging people to leave Earth for Mars, to move towards a more interconnected and, paradoxically, healthy reality. The Earth, partially contaminated by lethally toxic clouds, has lost many life forms, and its inhabitants, at least those who are still fully human, are forced to acquire robotic animals and plants to maintain a relationship with the other species that once populated the planet. Technology has pervaded every sphere of life and the boundaries between artificial prostheses and human tissues have been crossed. Several aspects of the book's plot are poignantly relevant to examining how the posthumanism theme relates to design.

Metamorphosis: From Myth to Posthuman Bodies

The first of these concerns metamorphosis, or the transformation of one being into another one of a different nature. This archetype is present in both Western and Eastern cultures, with variations that include, for example, transformations of inanimate matter into persons in the Shinto tradition (Amitrano et al.). But it is metamorphosis from human to plant, or from divinity to animal or human, that allows us to reason about the mythological archetypes that underlie our aesthetic tradition. Ovid's *Metamorphoses* has inspired much secular art, and also pop culture and music, nurturing and keeping alive the idea of a possible transmutation of living beings. Such ideas too are shapes that may be transformed: words that became images, images that became concepts, concepts that inspired research, research that turned into experiments.

The Emotional and Psychological Complexity of Androids

In Dick's novel the Nexus-6 are the *final* trial in this process: they are androids, a term derived from the Greek genitive of ἀνήρ (man) and the suffix -οειδής (of the species; similar), from εἶδος (appearance). Similar in appearance to humans, and thus in form, but constitutionally different, the Nexus-6 have learned to mimic needs, emotions and feelings but, unlike humans,' this set of characteristics comes from emulation, from a learning process that is not motivated by emotional characteristics endowed with consciousness.[1]

This observation appears, today, to be less outlandish than fifty years ago, as *deep learning*, part of the family of AI techniques, seeks to simulate the workings of the human brain; it involves increasing the speed and capacity of its predictions to enable computers to solve more complex problems (Herbrechter, *Posthumanism*). Today, AI has many subcategories, including neural networks, machine learning, computer vision and natural language processing, but it is often disembodied, tied to the cloud and artificial prostheses (mobile devices) rather than moulded to the template of our bodies. Yet when people consider the possible emergence of ASIs (artificial superintelligences), one of the most popular themes concerns their ability to replace obsolete and fallible humans, in the process acquiring a bodily appearance (Figure 1). With it come the first signs of that loss of control which underlies the disquiet that technology can produce: tension concerning hybridization and a sense that transformations are no longer managed by human beings (Badmington).

If myth has been the basis of our civilization, and if magic has played a role in human beings' daily lives, then even the most bizarre and frightening aspects of nature have found a raison d'être. Myth accommodates differences and maintains the degree of indefiniteness we need if we are to ponder the imponderable. But modern science has accustomed us to an exact system, a precise description of reality that avoids confusion. As long as science has

---

[1] The term "android" was mentioned by Albertus Magnus in 1270 and popularized by the French writer Villiers in his 1886 novel *Future Eve*, but it appeared in US patents as early as 1863, in reference to miniature toy automatons with human features. The female counterpart of the term android would be "gynoid," from the Greek γυνή (woman), but the masculine is more often used for both sexes.

governed technology, ensuring that it has remained an instrument in the hands of the rational, a form of balance has been maintained (Severino, *Nihilism and Destiny*).[2] If science is exact, if its purposes are clear and precise, and if we can evaluate the consequences of its findings, then humanity sleeps soundly. Following these premises, then, we accept technology as a gift and imagine the future as a better time in which humans will live long and serenely. This is the preamble that led to transhumanism and its ultimate goal of immortality.

Accordingly, the Nexus-6's transhuman nature and cyborg bodies are the novel's second aspect of interest. We find many synonyms for the term "androids", especially in science-fiction literature, where they are also called automatons or extraterrestrial creatures in human form, replicants, humanoids and cyborgs (Ballard). The physical similarity between humans and androids elicits a perturbing feeling, derived from the set of differences, imperceptible in the case of the Nexus-6, that define the human and non-human. The latter is perceived as "the other than oneself": the different, the foreign, even more insidious because it is unrecognizable. To see one's own image reflected in the android is to look at a hellish portrait, a will to power realized in the dual status of immortality and the absence of needs.

Figure 1. Image edited by the NABA Research Center, illustrating the evolution of technology for human beings.

---

[2] "This attitude is one of the determining factors that has lead humans beings outside of the existence guided by myth, where instead the context invades, overlaps and enmeshes itself with what is surrounded by it; and thus, where a thing can be many other things at one time: tree or animal, and at the same time demon; wind and voice of the gods; food and the vital force of the ancestors; earth fissure and maternal womb" (72).

Dick's novel reveals the dual drives of attraction and repulsion toward the *diabolical* humanoid: the androids the protagonist must kill are the same as the one he has fallen in love with. But why does Rick Deckard have to eliminate the Nexus-6? This "generation" of androids has an anomaly: they do not respond to the settings implanted in their memories but flee the Mars colony. Replicants, in short, do not behave like good robots but are unpredictable, bringing their behaviour dangerously close to human attitudes. Even science fiction cannot tolerate this latest metamorphosis, which threatens to make the machine the victor in its race with humans (Braidotti). The trajectory that has brought us to the domain of the sciences cannot be changed, and there is no longer room, it seems, for the magical and the uncanny.

Human-Technology Symbiosis: A New Paradigm

This leads to the novel's third aspect of interest: human beings' relationship with technology, which has ceased to be a tool in our hands and become a destiny toward which all of humanity tends (Heidegger). The Western theoretical tradition from Heidegger to Severino has analysed this process, which shifts the very foundations of civilization toward a relativism that hinges on *doing*, rather than *being*.[3] For many centuries the power of religions, embodied in sacred texts and rituals, traditionally contained the advance of technological power (Zolla, *Tradizione*). These fundamentals had already disappeared long before the first Industrial Revolution, and today are palely revisited in ethical issues (Battaglia et al.).

The most relevant metamorphosis is that of Daedalus and Icarus (Ovid). Tired of Cretan captivity and eager to return to Athens, Daedalus builds wings out of feathers and wax for himself and his son. During their flight, Icarus, despite his father's recommendations, gets too close to the sun and his wings melt from the heat; left without wings, the boy falls into the sea and dies. Icarus represents the contrast between ambition and measure, between excessive curiosity and restraint. The Greek concept of κατά μέτρον ("according to measure") as the path to serenity is expressed through the metaphor of flight:

---

[3] "Technique destroys the entire Western tradition by having at its foundation the téchne, that is, the way the Greeks think about human action. For them, at the root of all acting, human or divine, lies the becoming and the oscillation of things between being and nothingness. It is a matter of understanding that first in this thought, and then in the way it reaches its radicality in the technique of our time, lie the *"roots of violence"* (Heidegger 10–11, translated by the author).

neither too high (lest the sun burn you) nor too low (lest you drown in the sea). The metaphor of falling during flight brings us back to humans' dual relationship with animal and divine natures: neither bird nor God, humans need to transcend themselves, to transform themselves into something else, and probably to lose their *"humanity"* in order to make progress in discovering their potential (Ong). Not coincidentally, the flight of Icarus is the project of Daedalus, the first person to be called an "architect", in reference to the famous labyrinth of Minos. Project evolution and a loss of self-seem to intersect in this myth, which identifies metamorphosis with death, hubris with defeat. But who is Icarus in our original story? The inventor of the Nexus-6, or the hunter, or the androids themselves?

Art and the Posthuman Future: Foreshadowing Technological Evolution

This question leads us to the fourth observation about the novel: it is in literature and art that we find the most interesting examples foreshadowing, anticipating and inspiring those technological breakthroughs which critical posthumanism can encapsulate. It would be helpful to have clarity on terminology since, for several years now, we have been hearing about transhumans, posthumans and the post-Anthropocene without clear terminological distinctions. The *Encyclopaedia Britannica* gives this definition:

> transhumanism advocates the use of current and emerging technologies – genetic engineering, cryonics, AI, and nanotechnology – to augment human capabilities and conditions envisioning a future in which the responsible application of such technologies enables humans to slow, reverse, or eliminate the aging process . . . and humans with augmented capabilities will evolve into an enhanced species that transcends humanity – the posthuman.

Developments in science and technology make it possible to consider the very concept of human nature to be artificial, a product of an ideology that humanism has constructed and disseminated (Haraway). It would therefore be more accurate to speak of posthumanism than of the posthuman. In fact, whereas humanism makes the human being central and self-referential, its critics now question this, instead aiming to confront the otherness of a globalized world and to overcome anthropocentrism by recognizing animals' and technologies' contributions to hominization and cultural evolution (Hayles). The posthuman is a consequence of the leap that cultures have made from a dimension of *adaptation* to one of *expansion*: from a sphere of intervention limited to the material, external world to the possibility of directly influencing the genetic and biological dimensions of the human being (Marchesini). Advances in computer, biological and bioinformatic sciences and technologies have shown the possibility of overcoming the fleshy body, the frame which has always constituted the human being, in favour of more efficient (or even immortal) artificial supports, proper to a *new species* (Maurizi). This brings us from Frankenstein's monster to the cyborg, which combines organic and cybernetic parts and in which it is no longer possible to recognize any intact naturalness of the human being *ab origine*.

The whole weight of this metamorphosis is on the shoulders of those subjects (first humans, then androids or cyborgs) who transcend the use of prosthetics in favour of genetic and technological or neural mutation. Animals are still guinea pigs in many experiments, such as those conducted by Jeff Bezos' startup, Altos Labs. According to statements by the Spanish scientist Juan Carlos Izpisua, the experiments he conducted were based on the intermittent activation of four genes involved with rejuvenation. Izpisua and his team observed that mice with these genes activated, when their genetic aging was accelerated, lived up to 30% longer than their peers and exhibited rejuvenating effects on a wide range of tissues, with especially striking results in the skin and kidneys.[4]

Science fiction, in addition to imagining technological devices capable of this hybridization or mutation, has confronted us with the theme of our transience, the fragility with which we inhabit this planet, and the need to eliminate pain and, consequently, death. This is not an abstract thought; if we try to remember our experiences of pain then we immediately understand the power of this path (or escape?) to salvation. A fundamental aspect of religious traditions has been the relationship between death and accepting grief (Ariès), to the extent that death is a necessary passage to eternal life, an unavoidable threshold. Having lost this tradition and become immersed in the "power of technology," how can we relate to this absolute, if not by demanding answers from the very object that has distanced us from the tradition itself?[5]

---

[4] https://www.futuroprossimo.it/2022/03/altos-labs-rompe-il-silenzio-20-anni-e-potremo-prevenire-linvecchiamento%ef%bf%bc/.

[5] "Contemporary culture breaks free from tradition, and thus also from the religious tradition of the West, with a force that is peremptory and unstoppable, and essentially unknown to those

Figure 2. Black Mirror, "White Christmas" episode, TV series (2014).

How are we to overcome this impasse? One answer, it seems, is to turn the body into a machine, making our life itself so performance-efficient that we no longer need to fear death. Yet neither art nor design seems to be reassured by this post-eugenic possibility. On the contrary, dystopian visions are multiplying in popular culture: think of *Black Mirror*, which anticipated, almost eerily, the planetary pandemic (Figure 2). We can partly attribute this trend to the loss of purpose that more advanced technologies bring to users' attention. Machines are no longer made to fulfil a simple function. Generative AI, for example, no longer proceeds according to the pattern of progressive data entry, but has moved into the area of intuition and the association of ideas that, until now, has been the exclusive preserve of humans (at least according to the anthropocentric view of intelligence).

This brings us back to the existential dimension of the Nexus-6: today we face the possibility of designing androids similar to those described in the novel. The end of the illusion of machine control (understood here to be synonymous with technology) extends beyond bodies: it occupies social life, infrastructure and the remotest landscapes of Earth. Yet the physical spaces in which we live seem to interest us less; by now they have been falsified through the filters of social networks and augmented reality. The *Fight Club* protagonist's apartment, furnished entirely with IKEA pieces purchased online, has now evolved into space that is gamified, dematerialized and

---

who are its bearers. The waning of the immutable of Western tradition is inevitable, and thus the claim of traditional and religious culture to make a return to the past practicable is illusory" (Severino, *[short title]* 253, translated by the author).

transported to another universe (Figure 3). Transhumans and cyborg bodies, post-apocalyptic cities, implants and nanotechnologies are becoming more and more prevalent in life, as well as in art and design.

The space that contains these bodies is also divided: physical reality, immediately accessible to the five senses, is now contrasted with augmented or virtual reality and the Metaverse. For more than twenty years now, we have been analysing the state of megacities and global cities, exposing their limitations and dangers, so it is unsurprising that corrective attempts are being made, even at the spatial level, to beautify our living environment by recreating it in a virtual form without its disfigurements (Burdett). Yet the most recent innovations related to space seem more interested in bringing the Metaverse to physical places than the other way around. Two comparable examples are Google Glass and Apple Vision Pro. The first, designed by X Development, are glasses equipped with augmented reality. They allow users to view information as one would with a smartphone, but in "hands-free" mode, using voice commands instead of manual interaction. On the other hand, the Apple Vision Pro is described as Apple's first "space computer": a device that can integrate digital content with physical space.

Figure 3. David Fincher, Fight Club, film, 20th Century Fox, USA (1999).

Spatial Computing is a set of technologies that enable interaction between users and three-dimensional digital environments in an intuitive and natural way, using one's movement, voice and gaze. This concept focuses on integrating digital elements into the physical world, making the boundary between the two less and less perceptible: Spatial Computing extends physical reality by enriching it with information and interactive virtual objects. Unlike Apple's previous projects, this one does not unequivocally declare certain goals; it is an experiment that imagines what users and technology might develop together, opening up the possibility of integration with AI.

The Metaverse, on the other hand, is often described as a parallel digital universe: a persistent virtual world where users can meet, interact, work and play. Unlike Spatial Computing, which amplifies one's experience of the real world, the Metaverse is intended to offer an alternative to it, a fully immersive experience that exists independently of physical reality. Yet the Metaverse has failed to gain uptake; its immersiveness is limited, and the tools that could bring it closer to a full sensory experience are far from being available to generalist users. For example, HoloTile, conceived by Lanny Smoot, is a multidirectional platform, integrated into the floor without any attachment to the body, that can detect users' movements and then reproduce them in a virtual environment. It consists of several movable modules that, when placed below the feet, allow the user to walk in place. HoloTile allows multiple individuals to walk independently in different directions, and to move objects on the platform through a "gesture-based" interface. Smoot said:

> imagine a group of people in a room, able to be simultaneously elsewhere collaboratively. Imagine theatre stages equipped with these integrated devices, allowing dancers to perform extraordinary movements. . . . There are multiple applications for this technology, and we still don't know all the contexts in which it could be employed.[6]

Although Smoot's examples focus primarily on the entertainment industry and enterprise applications, it is not unrealistic to think of a more compact home version of HoloTile, aimed at VR visor users. The slow movement and high cost of the technology make it an unlikely substitute for a sunny cross-country run on a rainy day, but it is an interesting trend which may find uses in the event of extreme pollution.

Glasses that enable us to see beyond the limits of physicality were previously depicted in a 1991 film by Wim Wenders, *Until the End of the World*. Set at the turn of the millennium in the shadow of a world-changing catastrophe, the film follows a man and woman as they are pursued across the globe; the plot involves a device that can record visual experiences and

---

[6]   https://www.dday.it/redazione/48224/spostarsi-nella-realta-virtuale-camminando-davvero-ecco-il-pavimento-holotile-di-disney.

visualize dreams (Figure 4). This object closely resembles the above examples, as much in form as in its function, which is to record the most precious element of our humanity: memories. This is a collector of information that has escaped from the present but is fundamental to designing the future, making it poetic and lyrical but also sad and incoherent. The film reveals our obsession with images and technology in an age already completely globalized. The intercontinental landscape that Wenders presents is so precise and significant that it includes places that were planned but never realized, among them Jean Nouvel's Tour Sans Fins, soaring over the horizon in La Défense. A meta-narrative of our visual narcissism, today it seems more relevant than ever. Although technology has the power to transport us into a dimension of attractive possibilities, the original question remains: why do we want to desert our physical world? What is so limiting, scary and repulsive about it? For designers and architects, this question is crucial.

Figure 4. Wim Wenders, Until the End of the World, film, Warner Bros (1991).

Going back to our first example, the monumentally dystopian atmosphere of *Do Androids Dream of Electric Sheep?* is even better realized in the sets of the film that was based on Dick's book, thanks to the prodigious advances in technology that, again, offer powerful and immersive visual effects. The Los Angeles that appears in the first scene of *Blade Runner* (1982) makes concrete a century of fears and visions, simulations and catharsis. We need no longer interpret an author's words; images offer us a ready-made, unambiguous solution. The result of a refined process of knowledge that draws on such works as Fritz Lang's *Metropolis*, but also on *Star Wars*, Jean Giraud's comic books and the landscapes of *The War of the Worlds*, *Blade Runner* also offers us that perverse, playful pleasure of the Luna Park described in the pages of *Delirious New York*. Directed by Ridley Scott, the film's impressive post-apocalyptic vision directs our expectations of the future and defined the aesthetics of the technological dystopia for years to come (Figure 5). Its imaginary urban landscape was designed by Syd Mead, who explained that Scott wanted incredible congestion at street level, a *hybridization* of urban infrastructures, "so the streets are no longer simple places of transit as the housing dimensions exceed the possibilities offered by the simple use of the elevator".[7] This description concerns an imaginary world, conceived as a possible consequence of a series of irreversible human actions, because if good architecture begets beautiful ruins, then bad urban politics and bad economics beget horrible cities. The metropolis, in the twentieth-century imagination, is a living organism in which antagonistic principles coexist, or rather, fight.

Figure 5. Ridley Scott, Blade Runner, film, Los Angeles, Warner Bros (1982).

The Dystopian Cityscape: From *Blade Runner* to *Akira*

The same exponential growth, as if the city had become a concrete degenerate, is presented in *Akira* (1988), an animated cyberpunk action film from Japan (Figure 6). In the collective imagination, inspired both by the consequences of nuclear energy and by the society of the spectacle, the holding limit of a space

---

[7] https://scrapsfromtheloft.com/movies/blade-runner-interview-syd-mead/.

is somehow linked to the limit of its power. Once this limit is exceeded, and the saturation of this "bigness" is reached, the shapes *migrate or degenerate*. This mutation, which arises from the meeting of heterogeneous elements, is part of the discourse on critical posthumanism.

Figure 6. Katsuhiro Otomo, *Akira*, film, Tokyo, Toho (1988).

Figure 7. Clive Wilkinson, Google Headquarters, Mountain View, California, USA (2005).

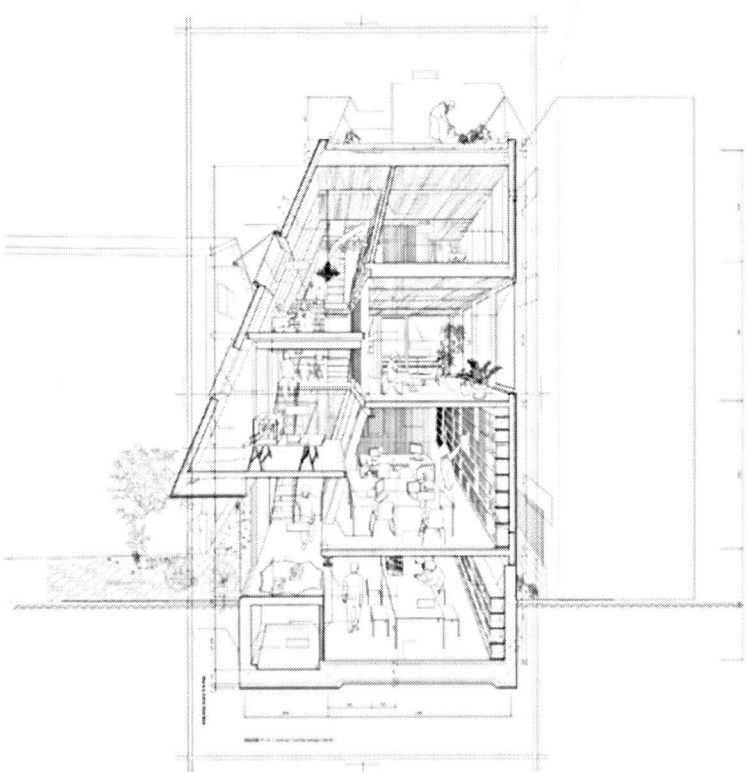

Figure 8. Atelier Bow-Wow, *House & Atelier* (section), Tokyo, Japan (2005).

The dystopian degeneration which people imagined in the Seventies and Eighties did not materialize, at least in the cities these films portray. On the contrary, San Francisco, Los Angeles and Tokyo represent places of advanced social innovation in which hybrid research involves the quality of the workplaces, from Clive Wilkinson's Google Headquarters in California to Atelier Bow-Wow's Office-house in Tokyo (Figures 7 and 8). Again, however, the smooth functioning of the interaction between heterogeneous elements, such as the classic modernist assumption of space for sleeping and space for working, is realized in the interior architecture: perhaps the smaller the space, the more successful the hybridization is.

An interesting new category that is replacing the canonical dimension of consumer places is that of data centres, fortified infrastructure built to protect one of the most ambiguous concepts in our society, namely privacy. In a recent Italian study, the journalist Annachiara Sacchi explored these "impassable fortresses, defended by armed guards and composed of miles of fiber, steel and cables" (Sacchi). These seemingly anonymous places manage millions of items of data – for companies, banks, hospitals, schools – and are noisy and extremely voluminous: the cloud, which in our imagination is an immaterial concept, needs gigantic spaces to operate (Figure 9). Politecnico di Milano's Digital Innovation Observatory describes the phenomenon as follows:

The Data Center infrastructure on the Italian territory represents a technological enabler for the delivery of services and solutions to support the digitalization of the country's enterprises. In recent years, the market has seen a growing interest, materialized in a conspicuous increase in investment and the opening of new infrastructure in Italy.[8]

Figure 9. Data Centre.

These buildings are not composed simply of volumes but of communication networks, energy and services. They need these to operate, maintain and, most importantly, protect the IT resources of small, medium and large enterprises alike. Data communication in 2024 requires the presence of enormous servers, for which Milan, Madrid, Zurich and Warsaw are the most interesting European cities, according to the Politecnico di Milano study. In their appearance we find no major differences from the canonical model of the twentieth-century factory; the change is in how they function as infrastructure. Madrid and Milan's proximity to the Mediterranean makes it possible to

---

[8] https://www.osservatori.net/it/ricerche/osservatori-attivi/data-center.

connect submarine cables to Africa and the Middle East, making them key providers of expertise and services to neighbouring countries: a geographic specialization linked to strategic factors that could change the territorial value of many areas.

This complexity requires a timely approach to the transformation of territories, as we can observe in two interesting examples from the multidisciplinary agency (Ab) Normal. *The Self Observing Landscape*, an ongoing project with the AA School, proposes an educational programme involving the construction of small digital landscapes, replicas of portions of physical territory. Starting with these fragments, large-scale three-dimensional maps can be developed (Figure 10). These digital simulations become tools for interpreting present social conditions and, simultaneously, for predicting the future. A new landscape emerges, able to observe itself through its prosthetic extension, its cybernetic twin.[9]

Meanwhile, the creative project *Ortigia Sound System* (2023) tries to envision the Sicilian territory's mutation by constantly looking at the past and simultaneously projecting into the future. Sicily is the centre of a network of ecological, geopolitical and cultural relations, close to the Mediterranean Sea. Imagining the future of Siracusa means speculating about how these transformations will affect the land and its populations. In 1869 the Suez Canal was opened, both drastically changing the surrounding ecosystem and transforming the use of the sea, and therefore greatly affecting Sicily. The island which will emerge in 2071 will give a new identity to this part of Italy, including desertification, rising sea levels, human migration and the colonization of certain animal species, and industrial and cultural transformation.[10]

These examples present a story with multiple endings: the possible consequences of anthropization appear alongside alternatives derived from the reasoned use of technologies. The use of space for storytelling through hybrid forms of analysis and design brings us back to the topic of generative Artificial Intelligences (GenAI) and websites that help users to produce text, images and music. Examples range from chatbots such as ChatGPT, developed by the OpenAI organization and capable of simulating a conversation with a human being, to Midjourney, which uses a bot integrated into a public channel on the Discord platform. Starting with image sets and text captions (such as Google's Imagen), one can shape new visual experiments, and this means continuously

---

[9] https://abnormalstory.com/TSOL.
[10] https://abnormalstory.com/OSS.

100   Elisa Poli

increasing the database of visual information available to AI. As Mario Carpo has illustrated, this process has many similarities to the idea of imitation typical of the Renaissance, showing how the opposition between humanism and posthumanism is in many ways inaccurate and misleading (Carpo).[11] The transformation of technology has a *programmatic* and *progressive* character for human beings today.

Figure 10. (AB)NORMAL, *The Self Observing Landscape*, AA Visiting School, On-going.

---

[11] In *Beyond Digital*, Carpo reviews the long history of the computational mode of production, showing how the merger of robotic automation and artificial intelligence will stop and reverse the modernist quest for scale. Today's technologies already allow us to use nonstandard building materials, either found or made, and to assemble them in as many nonstandard, intelligent, adaptive ways as needed: the micro-factories of our imminent future will be automated artisan shops.

Figure 11. Olivier Assayas, *Summer Hours*, Parigi, MK2 (2008).

In the 2008 film *Summer Hours*, Olivier Assayas tells the story of three brothers who, after the death of their mother, must sell the family home and its large collection of artworks. In the last scene, the family maid visits the now-empty house for the last time, and we catch a glimpse of the one object that, because it is worthless, has been left behind: an efficient satellite phone, abandoned on the windowsill. This filmic device shows the path of value that paintings and furniture have in the art market during the early 2000s and how, by contrast, that phone, which represents the most modern technology, turns out to be obsolete and meaningless (Figure 11). A small object, both affective and artistic before the camera, accompanies us as we consider what still has value for humans in the age of posthumanism, and in time and memory: the technology of everyday life, mass-produced, designed in one place and assembled in another, thousands of kilometres away, fades in the face of the richness of the original piece, a work of craftsmanship, an artistic artefact, with its unique and unrepeatable details and mistakes. A few fragments of an image encapsulate this theme: the value of human handwork in its originality and unrepeatability.

Other films have also represented the modern conflict between science, art and fate, the possibility of evolution through technology and the deep desire to maintain the primacy of human creativity as a sensitive and unique experience. Cinema has portrayed HAL 9000, the computer with a human-like personality in *2001: A Space Odyssey*; the artificial voice of Scarlett

Johansson in *Her*, a 2013 American science-fiction romantic drama film written and directed by Spike Jonze; and the lesser-known but superb first chapter of Krzysztof Kieślowski's *Dekalog: The Ten Commandments*, focused on the idolization of science: "I am the Lord thy God". Here the tragedy of a child's death results from a miscalculation by his father's computer. Faced with the vastness of the loss, looking at the lake into which his son has fallen because the ice covering it is thinner than his calculations had predicted, he exclaims: "It can't be, computers don't make mistakes" (Figure 12).

The point of view of this collective narrative has crumbled into a thousand more or less successful variations. At the centre of its perceptions, it always places human beings, who think, analyse, investigate, design, write, realize, interpret and judge. This is the story of human evolution produced by humans ourselves: the only animal species capable of thinking in the abstract and, in fact, of imagining itself. In conclusion, posthumanism is not a fantasy, a vague reverie of our intellect, but a rooted, tangible and recognizable epoch, verbalized by human beings but, soon, acted upon by machines. As W. H. Auden wrote in 1952, in his preface to a collection of fairy tales (Grimm et al.): "Every fairy tale teaches us not to tinker with our imaginative faculties; from fairy tale to fairy tale, we learn how wishing is a substitute for action; but desires, whether aimed at good or evil, are tremendously real and such that one cannot entertain them with impunity."

Figure 12. Krzysztof Kieślowski, *Dekalog: The Ten Commandments*, TV films (1988–89).

References

Amitrano G., Ki S. La metamorfosi come metafora letteraria nell'opera di Nakajima Atsushii. *Il Giappone*, vol. 23, 1983, pp. 157–185. *JSTOR*, https://www.jstor.org/stable/20750357.

Ariès P. *Essais sur l'histoire de la mort en occident: du Moyen Age à nos jours. Points*, 1975.

Badmington N. *Posthumanism*. London, Bloomsbury Academic; 2000.

Ballard J. G. *Hello America*. London, Cape; 1981.

Barthes R. *Mythologies*. Paris, Editions Du Seuil; 1957.

Battaglia F., Henry B., Pirni A. Ethics in Robotic and Intelligent Machines. *HUMANA.MENTE. Journal of Philosophical Studies*, vol. 16, 2023, pp. 3–5, https://www.humanamente.eu/index.php/HM/issue/view/46.

Benjamin R. *Searching for Whitopia: An Improbable Journey to the Earth of White America*. Vanves, Hachette Books; 2009.

Benjamin W. *Illuminations: Essays and Reflections*. New York, Schocken Books; 1968.

Brooker C. *Black Mirror*. Channel 4/Netflix, 2014–19.

Braidotti R. *The Posthuman*. Cambridge, Polity; 2013.

Burdett R. *Cities: Architecture and Society: 10th International Architecture Exhibition Venice Biennale*. Milano, Rizzoli, 2006.

Carpo M. *Beyond Digital: Design and Automation at the End of Modernity*. Cambridge, The MIT Press; 2023.

Cohen J. *Scènes de la vie future l'architecture européenne et la tentation de l'Amérique*. Paris, Flammarion; 1995.

Dick P. K. *Do Androids Dream of Electric Sheep?* London, Gollancz; 2010.

Douglas F., Collins C. *Celebration, USA.: Living in Disney's Brave New Town*. New York, Henry Holt and Co; 1999.

Ferraris M. *Documanità. Filosofia del nuovo mondo*. Milano, Laterza; 2021.

Fincher D. *Fight Club*. Fox 2000 Pictures; 1999.

Firebrace W. *Things Worth Seeing: A Guide to the City of W*. Savona, Black Dog; 1999.

Giedion S. *Mechanization Takes Command. A Contribution to Anonymous History*. Oxford, Oxford University Press; 1948.

Grimm W., Andersen H. C., *Tales of Grimm and Andersen*. New York, Modern Library Giant; 1952.

Haraway D. J. *When Species Meet*. Minnesota, University of Minnesota Press; 2008.

Hayles K. *How We Became Posthuman: Virtual Bodies in Cybernetics, Literature, and Informatics*. Chicago, University of Chicago Press; 1999.

Heidegger M. *The Question Concerning Technology and Other Essays*. New York, Harper and Row; 1977.

Herbrechter S. *Posthumanism: A Critical Analysis*. London, Bloomsbury Academic; 2013.

Herbrechter S. *European posthumanism*. London, Routledge; 2017.

Lyotard J. *The Postmodern Condition: A Report on Knowledge*. Minnesota, University of Minnesota Press; 1984.

Lyotard J. *The Inhuman: Reflections on Time*. Redwood City, Stanford University Press; 1991.

Marchesini R. *Beyond Anthropocentrism: Thoughts for a Post-Human Philosophy*. Milano, Mimesis; 2018.
Marin L. *Utopiques: jeux d'espaces*. Paris, Editions de Minuit; 1971.
Maurizi M. *Al di là della natura. Gli animali, il capitale e la libertà*. Anzio-Lavinio, Novalogos; 2011.
Ong W. J. *Orality and Literacy: The Technologizing of the Word*. London, Methuen; 1982.
Ovid *Metamorphoses*. Oxford, Oxford University Press; 2004.
Ritzer G. *The Mcdonaldization Thesis*. New York, SAGE Publications Inc.; 1998.
Severino E. *Pensieri sul cristianesimo*. Milano, Rizzoli; 1995.
Severino E. *Téchne. Le radici della violenza*. Milano, Rizzoli, 2010.
Severino E. *Nihilism and Destiny*. Milano, Mimesis; 2016.
Zolla E. *Storia del fantasticare*. Firenze, Bompiani; 1964.
Zolla E. *Che cos'è la Tradizione*. Milano, Adelphi; 1998.

Chapter 7

Towards New Forms of Visual Narrative: AIneid, Virgil's Aeneid in the Age of AI

Fabio Morotti[*]
IULM University, Milan, Italy

Abstract

The exponential development of artificial intelligence (AI) has profoundly affected the creative sector, inaugurating a new age of generative culture and providing artists, filmmakers and other professionals with innovative tools. This paradigm shift engenders a need to re-evaluate the techniques employed to construct visual narratives. In this context, this paper examines the AIneid, Virgil's Aeneid in the Age of AI, a video project that reimagines Virgil's classic Latin poem Aeneid using text-to-image (T2I) and image-to-video (I2V) generative processes.

The video invites viewers to reconsider the possibilities of storytelling in the age of AI and the profound effects that AI software and platforms can have on our understanding of literary texts. Furthermore, it provides an opportunity to reflect on the – perhaps temporary – constraints of AI in terms of videography, where, as in this case, it must currently be tailored to the precise requirements of archaeological accuracy.

Keywords: human-AI collaboration, AI-generated cinema, visual storytelling, film adaptation, Midjourney Aeneid

---

[*] Corresponding Author's Email: fabio.morotti@iulm.it

In: Computational Arts and Creative Products
Editor: Alessandra Micalizzi
ISBN: 979-8-89530-426-6
© 2025 Nova Science Publishers, Inc.

Introduction

The rapid development of artificial intelligence (AI) has significantly shifted the creative paradigm, ushering in a new kind of generative culture and providing powerful tools to users. The advent of generative AI software has affected the creative industry, especially those employed producing audio-visual and multimedia content. Ever-more artists, filmmakers and other specialists in both professional and non-professional contexts are drawn to using AI capabilities by the potential to significantly reduce the time and cost of content creation and are interested in broadening their creative and business horizons. Consequently, "traditional methodologies of video creation and storytelling are undergoing a profound transformation" (Masi and Di, 2024), necessitating reflection on the process (Baiheng and Wen, 2020).

This contribution examines the project that led to "AIneid, Virgil's Aeneid in the Age of AI" (3' 20"), a piece of audio-visual content that re-imagines the Aeneid, a classic of Latin literature written between 29 and 19 BC by the Roman poet Virgil[1]. The video was created by adapting the literary text via two of the most prominent applications of generative AI, text-to-image (T2I) and image-to-video (I2V), without relying on lens-based recordings of reality.

This project[2] was born of a partnership between the International Research Centre on Collaborative Translation[3] (IULM University, Milan) and Karma Lab (Koç University, Istanbul). It was conceived as part of the research intended to enhance and promote the cultural itinerary of the "Aeneas Route" (Aeneas Route - Cultural Routes, s.d.). From a theoretical standpoint, this video project was designed to examine the capabilities of the AI image and video generators that are currently available, focusing on Midjourney (Midjourney, n.d.) and Runway (Runway, n.d.). Furthermore, it was meant to facilitate a comprehensive examination of how, in the context of textual prompts, the generative processes of AI software and its interfaces "acting as representations" (Manovich, 2001: 40) are engendering a re-evaluation of the techniques of visual storytelling. Finally, this paper considers the influence of the selected AI software on the narrative of the video project and the

---

[1] For further insight into this literary masterpiece, see Camps (1969) and Williamson (2019).
[2] The author of this paper conceived and participated in the research as part of a doctoral programme in Visual and Media Studies (IULM University) and as a visiting researcher at Koç University.
[3] This project is part of the research program "AIneid, Narrating Mythology in the Age of AI".

development of its characters and visual style and reflects on the results of this research.

Methodologically, this project employed an auto-technographic and exploratory approach to examine the behind-the-scenes creation and learning process, focusing on pivotal moments in production. It combines elements of technography and autoethnography to understand the intersection between the researchers' personal experiences and the software technology employed. This was done to attempt to answer the following question: How do the specificity of the interfaces and their capabilities, coupled with the biases, occasional incoherence and technical constraints of AI software, influence the overall figuration and narration of the project?

The text-to-image generation process has been widely explored in the literature (Ahmad et al., 2024; D'Isa, 2024; Ding et al., 2022; Gafni et al., 2022; Ramesh et al., 2021). Numerous articles have been published exploring the characteristics of generative models (Esser et al., 2023) and text-to-video platforms (Guo et al. 2024; Karaarslan and Aydin, 2024; Kondratyuk et al. 2023; Wang et al., 2024). Several contributions also focus on the emerging field of AI-generated cinema (Danesi, 2024; Pradeep et al., 2023). This paper also considers contributions from non-academic sources, including bloggers and AI users (GreatAIPrompts, n.d.; Mickmumpitz, n.d; Nest, n.d).

The Choice of AI Video Generative Software

The research team surveyed the principal AI software and platforms currently available on the market (Gozalo-Brizuela and Garrido-Merchán, 2023). This included an analysis of Pika Lab (Pika, n.d.), Imagen Video (Ho et al., 2022), Stability AI (Stability AI, n.d.) and Kaiber (Kaiber, n.d.). The analysis led the research team to dismiss the hypothesis of creating a direct representation of the Aeneid with text-to-video technology. T2V models are still in the early stages (Gozalo-Brizuela and Garrido-Merchán, 2023: 8) and are currently unsuitable for complex narratives, such as that of the Aeneid, that require multitudinous shots, recurring characters and locations, or involve scene transitions. Instead, a double translation using T2I and then I2V was employed, although this method entailed a general loss of quality in the generated clips and a significant increase in the typical visual disturbances (mainly low stability and loss of photo-definition) that characterise AI cinematic figuration.

The exploratory phase preceding the selection of software was conducted with the awareness that the video production process would evolve, given a continuously changing technological landscape where new generative models, software and updated versions would emerge[4], rapidly making any previously employed software structurally obsolete. This was particularly true as video production occurred alongside the imminent, long-awaited advent of Sora OpenAI (OpenAI, 2024), which has been hailed as "the beginning of a new era in video generation" (Wang et al., 2024: 811).

The research team identified Midjourney V6 and Runway Gen-2, respectively, for the T2I and I2V translations to process the story and respect its archaeological and historical verisimilitude and accuracy requirements, despite these programs' inherent limitations. The ComfyUI (Yubin, 2023) user interface platform was also selected for its potential to significantly enhance performance and outcomes if the results obtained with Midjourney and Runway failed to meet expectations.

Midjourney is a software system that generates digital images with high aesthetic value from text inputs or web links. It was developed with the high-level programming language Python (Kuhlman, 2011). Midjourney was selected for the T2I generative stage of the project due to the physical user's degree of involvement, which is estimated to be the highest in Midjourney compared to other available software (Jaruga-Rozdolska, 2022: 97). This degree of engagement allowed the researchers to address the multitude of "errors" that emerged throughout the process. The software offers a wide range of tools and commands allowing users to interact more effectively with the T2I process and permitting the adoption of photographic language, encompassing elements such as camera angles and shots. The software was selected particularly for its capacity to alter specific regions of the generated images and utilise negative prompts (--no) and character references (--cref), which were crucial for the adaptation of the source text.

The T2I generative process with Midjourney can be outlined as: upon inputting the command "/imagine" and a series of keywords (known as prompts) the user is presented with four preliminary images, each derived from those inputs. If any of the images are of interest, they can be upscaled, developed further, or used to create additional variants. If the initial drafts fail to meet the user's expectations, they may repeat the process with the same

---

[4] While the research video project was finalised, the new, more powerful V3 of Runway, one of the platforms used in the project, was launched.

keywords or reformulate the prompt to obtain different results (Jaruga-Rozdolska, 2022: 97).

Runway Gen-2 was selected as the principal software for the I2V stage, in which images were used as prompts. Runway is a user-friendly platform that supports style transfer, image creation and expansion, camera movement and cinematographic language, motion tracking, scene detection and the integration of multiple plug-ins and other functions (Guo et al., 2023: 87). Furthermore, it includes lip-sync functionality, although the results of this function are constrained by certain input parameters (Runway ML, n.d.).

After testing the Runway Gen-2 tool for video generation from realistic images, the tool exhibited several challenges and some instability, particularly in handling character turns (Cui et al., 2024) and blurred areas or subjects in the input image. Therefore, the T2I process had to be adjusted to mitigate the effects of these constraints. Moreover, the dynamic range of the video is large, resulting in low stability, and using text prompts to support or delimit the I2V process appeared ineffective. As a recent comparative study (Guo et al., 2024: 90) affirmed, Runway's functionality appears "completely sufficient for non-professionals, but it needs better improvements for some professional video creators who need more sophisticated content".

However, upon inputting a given image Runway presented the option of using brush tools, allowing specific areas of the image prompt to be regulated and, thus, the movement of objects, animals and humans to be simulated, as well as facial expressions created. This possibility, combined with a realistic inclination in the generating process, was decisive in the final choice, although the features of certain competitors were occasionally superior or comparable (Guo et al., 2024).

ComfyUI (comfyanonymous, 2023) is a versatile graphical user interface (GUI) for stable diffusion that offers a node-based interface for complex multimedia tasks (Yubin, 2023). ComfyUI segregates workflows into customisable elements, allowing users to link various blocks to perform specific tasks. This offers various ways to fine-tune prompts to produce results that better reflect the user's intentions, such as up- and down-weighting specific parts of a prompt, loading a control point model, specifying a sampler, and more. One of ComfyUI's key benefits is its ability to help users track different versions of their images, control inputs and outputs and visualise the generation process without engaging in coding.

By effectively integrating ComfyUI, Runway and Midjourney, this project adopted a flexible workstream. However, the level of detail provided by ComfyUI may be excessive or daunting for the average user, who may not require insight into the intricate workings of generative AI (Charles, 2024: 60).

The Challenges of Achieving a Coherent Representation with AI Generative Software and Platforms

The advent of AI is stimulating the adoption of innovative workflows and methodologies for visual storytelling, largely due to the paradigm shift from rendering pixels to generating pixels (Curiosity Podcast, 2023) in image and video creation. Considering AI a "predictive medium", as the academic Lev Manovich (2023: 5) notes, implies the need to develop and implement new working models that can adapt to the largely random nature of the distinctive visual synthesis produced by AI generative processes. Moreover, when using AI platforms, users must consider and address various technical issues and challenges to create a coherent narrative and visualisation. This section will examine the process behind the creation of AIneid, Virgil's Aeneid in the Age of AI, to show how the chosen AI software affected the transposition of the literary source text. Several key aspects of the process will be emphasised, including historical mismatches, content policies, character creation and consistency across different shots and the challenge of placing multiple characters within a frame.

Disclaimer

Historical Mismatching

AI models are trained on datasets of contemporary images, which can bias their character representation, storytelling tropes and cultural narratives (Krasadakis, 2023). The training datasets used for AI models often comprise a vast number of images, but they may lack sufficient breadth to represent the full spectrum of historical eras accurately. Consequently, they cannot reliably depict historical objects, fashions and contexts that are not well-represented in the training data.

In the context of the myth of Aeneas and the fall of Troy, which is set around 1,200 BC (Strauss, 2007), the generated images demonstrated a notable absence of historical understanding of clothing and architectural features and forms. It prominently featured both Greek and Roman buildings from various periods, causing bizarre historical mismatches (see Figure 1).

Figure 1. Image produced by the prompt: Prompt: 1,200 BC, night, ancient Troy burning.

Figure 2. Image produced by a complex prompt specified in the footnote[5].

---

[5] Troy 1,200 B.C., Aeneas leans on a wall, Aeneas is in misery, night, very dark, mild burning city of Troy, seen from a flat roof, dark ambience, cinematic, realistic, blurry background, 1080 p --cref https://s.mj.run/D3of8Ty0RZM --ar 16:9.

The challenge of creating consistent, believable settings led the research team to select the episode in which the ghost of Creusa appears to Aeneas "among the city roofs" (Virgil, 2015, II. 730–795) to adapt. By situating the scene on the roofs, the visual representation of the burning city of Troy could be limited to a marginal, background portion of the frame (see Figure 2). This approach was complemented by several refinements of the textual prompts to ensure the plausibility of the results. This strategy offered a solution to the software's architectural bias and stereotypes, which could otherwise have generated incoherent and inaccurate locations.

The Censorship of Content Policies

Both Runway and Midjourney have established rigorous regulations (Runway ML. n.d.; Midjourney n.d.) governing depictions of violence, gore, injury, nudity and related imagery. These content policies can be crucial limiting factors and must be considered from the inception of a project. In the Aeneid, elements of violence are vital, as they are in epics and myths in the wider sense.

The following example illustrates how the project yielded a series of images (Figures 4 and 5) representing Aeneas sacrificing a bull to "the supreme king of the sky-lords" (Virgil, 2015, III. 19–68), despite the constraints imposed by content regulations. However, animating the images with Runway would not have been feasible. This issue was addressed by applying an editing effect. The inability to depict the slaughtering of the animal constrained the researchers to reshape the narrative by adding another shot (Figure 4) to make the story visually comprehensible.

Figure 3. Aeneas approaches the bull.

Towards New Forms of Visual Narrative 113

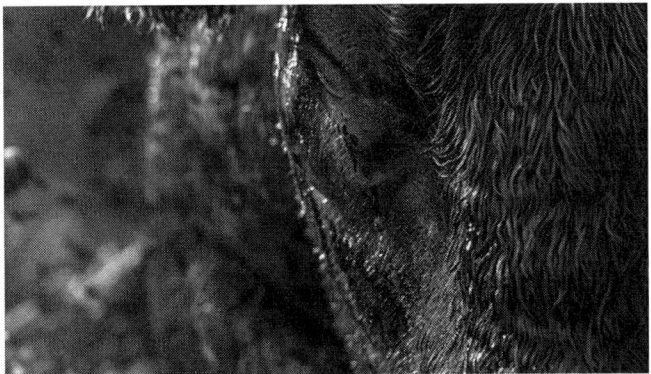

Figure 4. The sacrifice of the bull – very close-up.

Figure 5. The sacrifice of the bull – very close-up.

Figure 6. Polydorus' (non) transfixed body.

Figure 7. Polydorus' blood staining the earth.

As illustrated in Figure 6, the restrictions imposed on the content precluded the depiction of Polydorus's lifeless body being "transfixed" and "carpeted with spears" (Virgil, 2015, III.19–68). Instead, after multiple attempts, the animation of Polydorus' blood staining the earth was only achievable by darkening the fluid in the generated image (see Figure 7), a workaround that evaded Runway's content regulations.

Assessing the Photo Coherence of the Characters

When generating a character (Xi and Chung, 2023), it is important to assess photo-coherence to ensure that all visual elements, including facial expressions and anatomical proportions (particularly those of the hands and eyes), as well as lighting, shadows and textures, are consistent and realistic. Issues with photo-coherence can disrupt the overall cohesion and believability of the image, posing significant challenges to those who seek to achieve professional-grade digital storytelling and animations.

By drawing on the insights of experienced users (Kapoor, 2023; Nest, 2024) to enhance and optimise the predictability of the generation process with Midjourney, the research methodology for character creation involved certain elements of standardisation in the text prompts, with favourable outcomes. As shown in Figure 8, this entailed utilising a negative prompt, represented by the "--no" tag, at the conclusion of each input provided to address potential visual inconsistencies.

Figure 8. Image produced by the prompt specified in the footnote[6].

Figure 9. The young "Kevin Costner Aeneas" generated in one of the first image rounds with Midjourney[7].

To create the protagonist, Aeneas, the researchers employed a strategy of "fidelity" to the source text by seeking to identify aesthetic and physical references through a straightforward reading of the Aeneid. The descriptions derived from the literary text were reformulated and used in the prompts; some additional clues were incorporated while remaining faithful to the prevailing style and tone of specific scenes. The resulting images, however, demonstrated

---

[6] Prompt: 1,200 BC, Thracia, daylight, from top to down angle, close-up of the hand, field of wheat ears of wheat, hand on wheat ears, emphasize details like real skin, real hand, cinematic, very realistic, very detailed hand, high quality, 1080 p --no watermark, semi-realistic, render, sketch, cartoon, drawing, digital art, cropped, out of frame, low quality, blur, fake, bad anatomy --ar 16:09.

[7] Prompt: Aeneas, an ancient trojan man in armor, beautiful hair, joyful charmed eyes, noble face.

the presence of physical stereotypes and a bizarre resemblance to specific Hollywood stars (see Figure 9). Furthermore, the armour was incompatible with the archaeological record, recalling Roman-style, mediaeval or sixteenth-century forms that diverged from the stylistic norms of the intended era. Therefore, the researchers opted for a more flexible interpretation and sought to avoid creating overly stereotypical outcomes and circumvent the obstacle of representing realistic armour via a photo montage.

Recurring Characters in Different Shots

Building a visual story with a recurring character entails maintaining a consistent look and style across multiple frames. In general, using AI generation tools to adhere closely to a given visual reference is difficult. Before 13 March, when Midjourney introduced the --cref (character references) function, achieving character consistency across images was so challenging as to threaten the possibility of creating a professional visual story. In order to utilise the --cref tag, it is necessary to add it at the end of a prompt, accompanied by a URL to a previously generated image of the character. As shown in Figure 10, this feature allows the representation of a character, such as Aeneas[8], in a range of frames, scenes and settings. Therefore, the --cref tool offers significant benefits for narrative visual media such as films, novels and comic books, where consistent character appearances are essential.

In addition, Midjourney introduced the '--cw' (character weight) tag, which enabled users to specify a numerical value from 1 to 100 to indicate the weight of character consistency. However, the efficacy of this tool varies and is contingent on specific use cases and settings. Even at the maximum weight, the generation of some details is inconsistent, and when variations are created, the process remains highly random.

Even when the work is optimised with these tools and approaches, the reproduction of a character's details (decorations, clothes, specific physical features, such as moles, etc.) across images remains challenging and time-

---

[8] Aeneas sails aboard one of the boats built in Antandros. Prompt: https://s.mj.run/jvG2dudPj3c Aeneas is on board, an adult man, ancient trojan from 1200 BC, beautiful hair, joyful charmed brown eyes, noble face, eye contact, using a [14mm] lens, soft lighting style, cinematic, realistic, very detailed, 1080 p --no watermark, deformed iris, deformed pupils, semi-realistic, render, sketch, cartoon, drawing, digital art, text, cropped, out of frame, worst quality, blur, plastic, fake, uncanny valley, disfigured, deformed, bad anatomy --cref https://s.mj.run/NwBGuitj7rM --ar 16:09.

consuming. In terms of a visual narrative, this often leads users to adopt vague characterisations or employ post-production tools to enhance their results.

Figure 10. Image of Aeneas produced by the AI.

The Placement of Two or More Recurring Characters within a Frame

Consistent images of a single character are currently feasible with --cref. However, placing two or more recurring characters within the same frame presents significant challenges due to issues with contextual consistency, positioning and scaling. As Midjourney does not provide a specific tool for such visual narrative challenges, the results may be disjointed, with improperly overlapping characters that sometimes appear out-of-proportion or are lacking in natural interaction. To address these issues, detailed textual prompts in multiple iterations and with continuous adjustments are needed, yielding results that enhance the scene's overall realism. These techniques frequently yield unsatisfactory outcomes, however. From a narrative perspective, this precludes the construction of group scenes with recurring characters, necessitating the use of single-character shots instead.

During this research project, this limitation was encountered on several occasions and addressed in different ways. For example, the scene of Aeneas hugging the ghost of Creusa, which is a tragic and painful moment at the end of the second chapter of the Aeneid, was excluded after numerous attempts and unsatisfactory results. This prompted a re-evaluation of the narrative plan, which was reformulated to compensate for excluding the sequence.

Figure 11. Scene of Aeneas carrying his father Anchises on his shoulders and holding Ascanius' hand as he leaves Troy.

Another example is the well-known scene of Aeneas carrying his father Anchises on his shoulders and holding Ascanius' hand as he leaves Troy (Figure 11). The necessity for numerous iterations was a consequence of the presence of three characters, two of which (Aeneas and Anchises) were recurring. The desired outcome was ultimately realised only via post-production software.

Results and Conclusion

The audio-visual output produced only partially met the researchers' expectations for the project due to various factors, including technical constraints, inconsistencies, biases, content policies and regulations. To create audio-visual content that incorporates the precise details provided by literary sources, current software and platform limitations affect creators' aesthetic and narrative choices. In particular, some of the characters lacked sufficient detail and accessories, while the narrative was confined predominantly to shots that featured a single character. Furthermore, the overall story was constrained by strict temporal limitations and the difficulty of simulating action and natural movement, which gave the video adaptation the appearance of a tableau vivant.

To ensure the credibility of the images and clips produced by AI, the human element plays a pivotal role in the creative process, acting as a kind of "figurative checker". However, this process has proven exceedingly time-consuming, which counters one of the primary advantages of AI: its ability to speed production. To provide a comprehensive overview of the effort and amount of work involved in creating AIneid: Virgil's Aeneid in the Age of AI, some numbers may be useful. The video was produced in six months and comprised 2,500 images and 350 video clips. The final product, which consists of these elements, has a duration of just three minutes and twenty seconds.

From this perspective, considering the software employed in the project, notable improvements can be made in terms of characterisation quality, the precise delineation of specific areas within the frame and the streamlining and refinement of cinematic language processing. To progress towards more professional visual storytelling, this project suggests various potential enhancements that software developers might consider. The issue of representing multiple recurring characters in a single frame could be addressed by refining and numbering the Midjourney --cref tag, thereby clarifying the references and textual prompts for each character. Moreover, the implementation of a shot/reverse shot tool could prove advantageous, particularly in terms of time efficiency and usage in conjunction with the film technique known as "eyeline match". Runway could be developed to automatically determine suitable camera shots (e.g., very close-up, close-up, medium shot, long shot, etc.) and angles when generating videos from image prompts without the need to include such information in the textual prompts.

Another area of potential improvement is text-to-video functions. For T2V to be utilised effectively in a complex storytelling context where characters and locations recur, new working tools must be designed to guarantee coherence across different shots. Otherwise, AI will likely continue to be employed in conjunction with other filming and animation techniques and, thus, remain the domain of professionals. Although they do not currently attain the desired performance levels, recent developments in generative models (as showcased by Sora) have demonstrated potential for significant advancement (Wang et al., 2024: 813). The integration of multimodal data and the accessibility of more comprehensive datasets provide a promising foundation for the future of AI-based video generation. This could revolutionise the creative industry, reducing its reliance on physical shooting, scene construction and special effects, offering a cost-effective alternative to traditional video production.

Following the trends delineated by digital cinema, it is conceivable that it will soon be impossible to distinguish between the films or parts thereof that have been recorded with cameras and those that have been generated using AI. According to Cristóbal Valenzuela, the CEO of Runway, the term "AI" itself will slowly disappear as the technology becomes mainstream, and this transition will lead to the emergence of a completely new as-yet-unnamed artistic genre (Gleeson, 2022). This will further the disassociation of the physical relationship between video and reality that began with digital cinema (Manovich, 2016).

In conclusion, this project leads us to propose that we are currently witnessing the advent of a novel phase that may be characterised as a pre-cinematic AI era. As in the early days of cinema, we are currently witnessing the pioneering enthusiasm and pleasure of achieving natural, lifelike results (Neale, 1985) from AI figuration. Consequently, the predominant focus of most of the current efforts is on achieving verisimilitude, photographic credibility and the two-dimensional illusion of space and movement.

References

Aeneas Route. *Cultural Routes (n.d.). Available from:* https://www.coe.int/en/web/cultural-routes/aeneas-route-4.

Ahmad IS, Siddiqui N, Boufama B. A comparative study of text-to-image generative models. *2024 IEEE 12th International Symposium on Signal, Image, Video and Communications (ISIVC)*, (2024): 1–6. *Available from:* https://doi.org/10.1109/ISIVC61350.2024.10577779.

Baiheng L, Wen Z. Rethinking of artificial intelligence storytelling of digital media. *2020 International Conference on Innovation Design and Digital Technology (ICIDDT)*. Zhenjing, China (2020): 112–115. *Available from:* https://doi.org/10.1109/ICIDDT52279.2020.00029.

Camps WA. *An introduction to Virgil's "Aeneid"*. Oxford University Press, 1969.

Charles R. *Generative AI methods to create comic strips [MA thesis]*. Université de Liège; 2024.

Curiosity Podcast. *The future of generative AI video with Cristóbal Valenzuela, CEO and co-founder of Runway. Curiosity's Substack (2023).* Available from*:* https://curiositypodcast.substack.com/p/the-future-of-generative-ai-video.

comfyanonymous. *Github. Com-comfyanonymous-comfyui_-_2023-12-04_17-57-46* [Software] (2023). Available from: http://archive.org/details/github.com-comfyanonymous-ComfyUI_-_2023-12-04_17-57-46

Cui Y, Shan X, Chung J. A feasibility study on RUNWAY GEN-2 for generating realistic style images. *International Journal of Internet, Broadcasting and Communication (2024) 16(1): 99–105.* https://doi.org/10.7236/IJIBC.2024.16.1.99.

Danesi M. AI-generated cinema. In Danesi M. (Ed.), *AI-generated popular culture*. Cham: Palgrave Macmillan; *2024: 45–65.* https://doi.org/10.1007/978-3-031-54752-2_3.

Ding M, Yang Z, Hong W, Zheng W, Zhou C, Yin D, Lin J, Zou X, Shao Z, Yang H, Tang J. Cogview: Mastering text-to-image generation via transformers. *ArXiv, Cornell University* (2021). Available from: https://doi.org/10.48550/ARXIV.2105.13290.

D'Isa F. *La rivoluzione algoritmica. Arte e intelligenza artificiale [The algorithmic revolution. Art and artificial intelligence]*. Bologna: Luca Sossella Editore; 2023.

Esser P, Chiu J, Atighehchian P, Granskog J, Germanidis A. Structure and content-guided video synthesis with diffusion models. *2023 IEEE/CVF International Conference on Computer Vision (ICCV) (2023): 7312–7322.*

Gafni O, Polyak A, Ashual O, Sheynin S, Parikh D, Taigman Y. Make-a-scene: Scene-based text-to-image generation with human priors. In Avidan S, Brostow G, Cissé M, Farinella GM, Hassner T. (Eds.), *Computer vision – ECCV 2022 13675*, Cham: Springer Nature Switzerland (2023): 89–106. Available from: https://doi.org/10.1007/978-3-031-19784-0_6.

Gleeson C. Cristóbal Valenzuela, CEO of Runway, on rethinking the primitives of video. Sacra (2022, March 18). Available from: https://sacra.com/research/cristobal-valenzuela-runway-business-video-primitives/.

Gozalo-Brizuela R, Garrido-Merchán EC. A survey of generative AI applications. *ArXiv, Cornell University* (2023). Available from: https://doi.org/10.48550/ARXIV.2306.02781.

Great AI Prompts—*AI prompts, AI tools and AI news* (2023, May 1). Available from: https://www.greataiprompts.com/.

Guo B, Shan X, Chung J. A comparative study on the features and applications of AI tools – Focus on PIKA Labs and RUNWAY. *International Journal of Internet, Broadcasting and Communication, (2024) 16(1): 86–91*. Available from: https://doi.org/10.7236/IJIBC.2024.16.1.86.

Ho J, Chan W, Saharia C, Whang J, Gao R, Gritsenko A, Kingma DP, Poole B, Norouzi M, Fleet DJ, Salimans T. *Imagen video: High definition video generation with diffusion models Arxiv*, Cornell Univerity (2022). Available from: https://doi.org/10.48550/ARXIV.2210.02303.

Jaruga-Rozdolska A. Artificial intelligence as part of future practices in the architect's work: MidJourney generative tool as part of a process of creating an architectural form. *Architectus*, (2022) 3(71): 95-104. *Available from:* https://doi.org/10.37190/arc220310.

Kaiber. Available from: https://kaiber.ai/.

Kapoor M. *45+ best Midjourney prompts to try out. Great AI Prompts (2023, January 13). Available from:* https://www.greataiprompts.com/imageprompt/midjourney-text-to-image-ai-prompts/

Karaarslan E, Aydın Ö. *Generate impressive videos with text instructions: A review of OpenAI Sora, Stable Diffusion, Lumiere and comparable models (2024).* Available from: https://doi.org/10.36227/techrxiv.170862194.43871446/v1.

Kondratyuk D, Yu L, Gu X, Lezama J, Huang J, Schindler G, Hornung R, Birodkar V, Yan J, Chiu MC, Somandepalli K, Akbari H, Alon Y, Cheng Y, Dillon J, Gupta A, Hahn M, Hauth A, Hendon D, ... Jiang L. Videopoet: A large language model for zero-shot video generation. *ArXiv, Cornell University* (2023). Available from: https://doi.org/10.48550/ARXIV.2312.14125.

Krasadakis G. *The ethical concerns associated with the general adoption of AI*. Medium (2023, 2 November). Available from: https://medium.com/60-leaders/the-ethical-concerns-associated-with-the-general-adoption-of-ai-ab893e9b5196.

Kuhlman D. A Python book: Beginning Python, advanced Python, and Python exercises. *Platypus Global Media*; 2011.

Manovich L. *The language of new media (2001)*. Available from: http://dss-edit.com/plu/Manovich-Lev_The_Language_of_the_New_Media.pdf.

Manovich L. What is Digital Cinema?. In Denson S, Leyda J. Post-Cinema. *Theorizing 21st-Century Film*. Falmer: REFRAME Books (2016): 20-50.

Manovich L. *AI image and generative media: Notes on ongoing revolution. In* Manovich L, Arielli L. (Eds.), *Artificial aesthetic: A Critical Guide to AI, Media and Design* (2023). Available from: http://manovich.net/index.php/projects/artificial-aesthetics-book.

Masi VD, Di Q. *AI and the future of cinema: The transformative impact of our T2 remak*. LAB Research; 2024.

Mickmumpitz. *Mickmumpitz—Youtube*. Available from: https://www.youtube.com/@mickmumpitz.

Midjourney. Available from: https://www.midjourney.com/home.

Midjourney. *Community guidelines*. Midjourney Documentation. Available from: https://docs.midjourney.com/docs/community-guidelines?ref=yon.fun.

Neale S. *Cinema and technology*. Bloomington: Indiana University Press; 1985.

Nest D. Midjourney consistent characters (How to use --cref) *Why Try AI* (2024, March 14) Available from: https://www.whytryai.com/p/midjourney-consistent-characters.

OpenAI. *Sora: Creating video from text* (2024, February 15). Available from: https://openai.com/index/sora/.

Pika. Available from: https://pika.art/home.

Pradeep A, Satmuratov A, Yeshbayev I, Khasan O, Iqboljon M, Daniyor A. The significance of artificial intelligence in contemporary cinema. *2023 Second International Conference on Trends in Electrical, Electronics, and Computer Engineering (TEECCON)* (2023): 111–116. Available from: https://doi.org/10.1109/TEECCON59234.2023.10335867.

Ramesh A, Pavlov M, Goh G, Gray S, Voss C, Radford A, Chen M, Sutskever I. Zero-shot text-to-image generation. *ArXiv, Cornell University (*2021). Available from: https://doi.org/10.48550/ARXIV.2102.12092.

Runway. *Runway - Advancing creativity with artificial intelligence*. Available from: https://runwayml.com/.

Runway *AI Film Festival*. Available from: https://aiff.runwayml.com.

Runway Research. *Gen-2 by Runway* Available from: https://research.runwayml.com/gen2.

Runway ML. *Lip Sync. Runway Help Center*. Available from: https://help.runwayml.com/hc/en-us/articles/27286560189075-Lip-Sync.

Runway ML. *Why is my input getting content moderated, and what types of content are blocked? Runway ML Help Center*. Available from: https://help.runwayml.com/hc/en-us/articles/21745792516371-Why-is-my-input-getting-content-moderated-and-what-types-of-content-are-blocked.

Stability AI. *Available from:* https://stability.ai.

Strauss B. *The Trojan War: A new history.* New York: Simon & Schuster; 2007.

Virgil. *Aeneid (*A. S. Kline, Trans.). Roman Roads Media (2002).

Wang F, Miao Q, Li L, Ni Q, Li X, Li J, Fan L, Tian Y, Han Q. When does Sora show: The beginning of TAO to imaginative intelligence and scenarios engineering. *IEEE/CAA Journal of Automatica Sinica* (2024) 11(4): 809–815. Available from: https://doi.org/10.1109/jas.2024.124383.

Williamson, M. Virgil's *Aeneid*: The cornerstone of Roman identity. *Tenor of Our Time* (2019) 8: 159–171.

Xi C, Chung J. A study on character design using [midjourney] application. *International Journal of Advanced Culture Technology* (2023) 11(2): 409–414. Available from: https://doi.org/10.17703/IJACT.2023.11.2.409.

Yubin. *Beginner's guide to comfyui for Stable Diffusion. AiTuts (2023)* Available from: https://aituts.com/comfyui/.

Chapter 8

Conversational Artificial Intelligence and Autobiographical Writing

Lara Balleri[*]
and Francesco Epifani[†]
Università Telematica Pegaso, Naples, Italy

Abstract

According to Jerome Bruner, narrative is a fundamental form of human thought and communication; through stories, individuals understand their actions, interpret emotions, and make sense of their behaviors. Language, mainly writing, imbues autobiography with a reflexivity essential for constructing the Self, a continuous and unceasing process (Bruner, 2002). Through autobiographical writing, specifically focusing on the relationship between the writers and their names and how such relationship has evolved, one accesses events recorded as memories; practicing autobiography fosters a deeper understanding of one's motivations, contributing to constructing one's personal life project (Batini F., Del Sarto G., 2015). This research aims to employ narrative criteria associated with self-awareness to analyze the content of a corpus of autobiographical texts using tools like ChatGPT and MAXQDA 24, comparing the results yielded by these devices. In modern research on artificial intelligence and creativity, the role of advanced tools like ChatGPT has become increasingly central. These technologies are used for data and text analysis and demonstrate significant potential in creative production. This methodological chapter explores how ChatGPT can be

---

[*] Corresponding Author's Email: lara.balleri@unipegaso.it
[†] Corresponding Author's Email: Francesco.epifani@unipegaso.it

In: Computational Arts and Creative Products
Editor: Alessandra Micalizzi
ISBN: 979-8-89530-426-6
© 2025 Nova Science Publishers, Inc.

employed in these two capacities, demonstrating that a technology that generates creative content can also be a powerful analytical tool.

Keywords: autobiography, proper name, content analysis, ChatGPT, MAXQDA 24

Introduction

Artificial intelligence (AI) technologies, such as ChatGPT, offer an extraordinary opportunity to create synergy between content production and analysis. The same advanced capabilities that allow ChatGPT to generate creative texts can be leveraged to analyze and understand these same contents (Reiter E. & Dale R., 1997). This dual use represents a significant advancement in research and creativity. On the one hand, ChatGPT can be employed to produce original content, utilizing machine learning algorithms to generate texts ranging from stories and poems to scripts and academic articles. Its ability to understand context and deliver coherent and relevant texts makes it a functional tool for authors and content creators, as it can suggest ideas, propose narrative developments, and even overcome writer's block by providing stimulating phrases and paragraphs.

On the other hand, ChatGPT can be used for content analysis, as exemplified in this chapter, due to its natural language-processing capabilities, which allow it to examine existing texts to identify narrative structures, recurring themes, and thematic coherence. This tool can perform quantitative content analysis, including keyword frequency, and qualitative analysis, such as assessing texts' reflective depth and logical coherence.

The synergy between production and analysis becomes evident when we consider that the texts generated by ChatGPT can be immediately analyzed to assess their quality and coherence. This cycle of production and analysis allows for rapid content improvement, as insights derived from the analysis can be used to refine text generation further. For instance, an author can use ChatGPT to generate a first draft, have the chatbot analyze it to identify inconsistencies or areas for improvement, and then act on the analysis results to perfect the text. This integration between production and analysis speeds up the creative process and makes it more robust and informed; authors can obtain immediate feedback on their texts and make real-time adjustments, improving the quality of their work and maintaining focus on each step. Moreover, using ChatGPT for those two phases ensures the perpetuation of stylistic and thematic coherence, which might otherwise be compromised by using separate tools for production and analysis or allowing too much time to pass between the author's writing and their return to the text.

Adopting AI like ChatGPT for content production and analysis facilitates the generation of innovative content. It provides the tools for a deep understanding and critical evaluation of these contents, enhancing the two phases of the creative process. In a context like the one we will delve into below, once content analysis is performed on autobiographical texts, ChatGPT's generative value could express itself in the feedback it can generate in light of the analysis results. It could support the author by suggesting textual passages they wrote hastily and deserve further reflection and contribution or by recognizing the self-awareness reflected in their written words. This initial research will satisfy some of these needs, laying the foundation for a concrete subsequent in-depth study.

Autobiographical Narrative

According to Jerome Bruner (1915–2016), narrative is fundamental to human thought and communication. A pioneer in the study of narrative and the construction of meaning, Bruner argues that narratives focus on understanding human experiences, helping individuals comprehend their actions and intentions, interpret their emotions, and make sense of their behaviors. "Narrative structures organize experience and memory and guide action. They serve as a tool for making sense of the world, for communicating that sense, and for transforming it into a shared and communal understanding" (Bruner J. S., 2013). Thus, language serves as the medium through which thought occurs and evolves. Writing, particularly, endows language with a reflexivity essential for constructing the Self, an endless and uninterrupted process (Bruner J. S., 2002).

The autobiographical method is a powerful tool for self-creation and self-discovery, as it is a product of our storytelling rather than an essence to be unearthed from the depths of subjectivity (Bruner J., 2002). The autobiographical writing process allows individuals to attribute order and personal, emotional, and chronological hierarchy to events recorded as memories. "We constantly construct and reconstruct ourselves to meet the needs of the situations we encounter, and we do so with the guidance of our memories of the past and our hopes and fears for the future" (Bruner J. S., 1992). This process can lead to a deeper understanding of one's motivations, concretely contributing to constructing one's life project. "In the end, we become the autobiographical narratives by which we *tell about* our lives. And given the opportunity to narrate, we try to make our lives into a coherent and continuous story" (Bruner J. S., 2020).

Based on these theoretical premises, this research aims to identify a set of narrative criteria to detect the self-awareness exhibited by the author of each text, which is simultaneously generated for the author in and through the act of writing.

Four main criteria were envisioned: Narrative Structure (S01), Temporal Continuity (S02), Thematic Coherence (S03), and Integration of Experiences (S04).

Specifically, Narrative Structure traces the narrative coherence of a text, considering it in three ordered phases: beginning, development, and conclusion. Since Bruner posits that language, particularly narrative, is a means through which individuals construct reality, the ability to organize and present ideas and experiences sequentially demonstrates a disciplined and self-aware mind.

Similarly, although with nuances, Temporal Continuity is the evidence of a precise thought process that critically examines past experiences, considers present ones, and projects into the future. Conceiving oneself along a timeline demonstrates logical thinking; thus, temporal progression indicates that the author has conscious control over their narrative.

Thematic Coherence, in its capacity to construct a coherent and meaningful narrative, is a sign of self-awareness; a written text that expresses reflective passages and an understanding of one's experiences and ideas supports the thesis that writing contributes to and embodies self-awareness.

The narration of self, being not only a way to tell stories, serves as a method to make sense of experiences and construct a deeper understanding of oneself and the world; the narration of these experiences reflects the Integration of Experiences through relationships that may be continuous, contrasting, or otherwise.

Methodological Considerations

The research framework is defined by the theoretical background introduced. Establishing and using a set of categories for content analysis is not aimed at testing the robustness and validity of the construct from which we started but rather at comparing the functioning of two different devices in the quantitative analysis of content based on the same analysis categories to which appropriate keywords have been assigned. Although it could have been possible to identify random categories with no theoretical basis, the research presented here had to pedagogically characterize the premises from which a more circumscribed action originates despite being part of the process of literacy and experimentation with the use of computational artificial intelligence in social sciences. Notably, a solely quantitative analysis would not have met the research objectives even if the proposed model's validity for evaluating the level of self-awareness expressed by the autobiographical texts had been demonstrated.

The research question fueling this study is the possibility of evaluating comparable results and, consequently, the management methods of the related processes between content analysis performed using AI and that performed with common content analysis software typically used in sector-specific research. Specifically, the supposed opportunity offered by AI to process a large number of data has made it interesting for the authors to probe the reliability of the results obtained to evaluate the effectiveness of ChatGPT as a tool for quantitative content analysis available to researchers. Therefore, comparing content analysis performed by an AI chatbot with that performed by a non-AI content analysis software was the subject of the experimentation undertaken with the idea of making it reliable by ensuring some common elements for the two tools:

- adhering to the same analysis methodology (quantitative content analysis),
- working on the same corpus of autobiographical texts (173),
- using the same keyword dictionary.

Preliminary Research Actions and Reflections

Students enrolled in the degree programs Sciences and Techniques of Education and Services for Early Childhood and Psychological Sciences of Human Resources, Organizations, and Enterprises at the Telematic University IUL during the Academic Year 2022/2023 were asked to produce an autobiographical text expressing the value of their name and how their relationship with it has evolved over their lives. The intent is to embrace the proper name as a technology of the self (Foucault M., 1992), thus as an object of practice to achieve a different state, in this case, of awareness of lived experiences. These practices include meditation, confession, introspection, and other forms of self-reflection and self-discipline. Autobiographical writing conducted through the first name demonstrates great narrative potential in effectively responding to the need to immortalize the plurality of the subject's personality with characteristics of freedom, depth, and reflexivity, drawing from various situations and evolutions (Messuri I., Balleri L., 2024).

At the start of the preliminary data analysis activities, 173 autobiographical texts in Italian were included, constituting the corpus of texts on which the research was based. In these texts, spelling and typing errors were manually corrected, and images and clipart were removed. After identifying the most appropriate keywords for each category, their presence in the research corpus was verified until the most common ones were selected. At the end of this process, a set of keywords for each category was obtained, considered relevant to the analysis criteria and valuable as a keyword set for comparing the two devices.

ChatGPT version 4o was selected as the AI chatbot and MAXQDA 24 as the content analysis software. The preliminary activities necessary to proceed included installing MAXQDA 24, activating the license, and subscribing to ChatGPT Plus with access to Chatbot ChatGPT-4o (Omnia). This version claims superior performance to ChatGPT-4, updated in May 2024. The files were uniformly renamed (sequential number + author's first name) and imported into the program as separate files to perform the analysis with MAXQDA 24. An analysis dictionary was created based on the identified keywords; the software was then requested to code the texts automatically, and the generated codes were explored by activating the 173 imported texts. The resulting spreadsheets (in .xls format) were exported.

For the ChatGPT analysis, the phrases "inizio testo" and "fine testo" were inserted at the beginning and end of each autobiographical contribution, and a single file with the texts to be analyzed was created. The corpus was imported, and the correspondence of the number of texts detected in the file by ChatGPT was verified. The dictionary exported from MAXQDA with codes and keywords was imported, and a quantitative content analysis of the corpus was requested based on the imported dictionary. The outputs provided in spreadsheets were optimized with a series of requests until a fully functional set of files was obtained for comparison. The dictionary exported from MAXQDA was used for convenience; however, providing ChatGPT with an

Excel file containing criteria and keywords would have been identical, emphasizing the certain independence of one device from the other.

While loading the autobiographical texts into MAXQDA was very quick and error-free, the same operation on ChatGPT required several text adjustments to address several processing issues. Specifically, ensuring that the ongoing analysis was performed on the same number of loaded texts was necessary, as the results initially appeared suspicious. A single text file was created by merging all the autobiographical texts since loading the corpus of individual texts generated errors in their reading, causing some to be overlooked. Additionally, the "inizio testo" and "fine testo" indications were modified to include symbols for more certain recognition by ChatGPT, changing to "***start text***" and "***end text***" in the English version to avoid matching the same words, even without symbols, within the Italian text. This method ensured the inclusion of all texts intended for upload.

Consistency was maintained between the two groups of texts to compare the text analysis results, each renamed with sequential numbering associated with a proper name. Difficulties encountered with ChatGPT were resolved that way since finding the same names repeated multiple times was considered problematic. Based on the actions reported thus far, working with ChatGPT is considered more labor-intensive due to the necessary optimization of the material to be analyzed.

Analysis Results

After exporting the files from the analysis devices (MAXQDA vs. ChatGPT), a consistency analysis of the Criteria for each section was conducted. Specifically:

- S01: Presence of all variables indicated in the Declaration
- S02: Presence of all variables indicated in the Declaration
- S03: Presence of all variables indicated in the Declaration
- S04: Presence of at least four out of six variables indicated in the Declaration

This approach ensured the thorough examination of each criterion's consistency, providing a clear comparison between the traditional content analysis software and the AI-powered ChatGPT. The results of the analysis are reported in Table 1.

Table 1. Quantitative Analysis Results

ID	Section	Declaratory	Criterion	MAXQDA 24	ChatGPT-4o	Coincidence	Delta
S01	Narrative Structure	Beginning, Development, Conclusion	Presence of all variables	16	23	16	70%
S02	Temporal Continuity	Before, During, After	Presence of all variables	43	153	43	28%
S03	Thematic Coherence	Self-efficacy, Self-awareness, Understanding of experiences	Presence of all variables	7	130	7	5%
S04	Integration of Experiences	Concessive relations, Comparative relations, Conditional relations, Contrast relations, Additive relations, Temporal continuity	Presence of an absolute majority of variables (4/6)	49	62	49	79%

The results highlight the following key points, demonstrating the validity of using ChatGPT in quantitative content analysis:

1. MAXQDA, ChatGPT never ZERO: The research never produced an empty list.
2. Differences in analysis are generated from the same elements (Corpus of texts, Criteria, Keywords).
3. MAXQDA << ChatGPT: This supports the regularity and consistency of the analysis; we are comparing two different tools (the first technical and validated, the second continuously improving). The mathematical space (X) existing (MAXQDA < X < ChatGPT) will be the subject of further investigations.
4. MAXQDA is always properly included in ChatGPT: ALL results obtained on MAXQDA are always present in ChatGPT, indicating that ChatGPT certainly identifies all the results determined by MAXQDA but not only those. Hence, it becomes necessary to investigate the finite subset (ChatGPT - MAXQDA) to measure the precision of the analysis conducted by the tools and to encode, if the subset contains only errors, new instructions for ChatGPT to make the result appropriate.

For **S01 Narrative Structure**, the difference arose because ChatGPT detected and counted partial matches. For example, for "*ora*", terms like "anc*ora*", "Eleon*ora*", "Aur*ora*", "col*ora*" or "ad*ora*to" were counted. Similarly, the analysis erroneously included "d*alla fine*stra" based on the "alla fine" keyword.

For **S02 Temporal Continuity**, erroneous results were common due to the presence of the keyword "*ora*" detected within other terms like "inc*ora*ggiato" "ad*ora*to", which are irrelevant to the category.

For **S03 Thematic Coherence**, the difference was attributable to the same dynamic observed in S01, for keywords like "*so che*" detected within terms like "spes*so che*".

For **S04 Integration of Experiences**, the difference was due to ChatGPT counting some subcategories that did not include relevant terms, identifying the presence of four out of six parameters in many texts.

Conclusion

The two tools used demonstrated the ability to identify a common base of resources: each MAXQDA 24 result set is finitely included in the ChatGPT result set. The latter exposes a subset of results (the difference) attributable to errors in identifying the correct quantitative sample. This means that ChatGPT can perform the work of MAXQDA 24 comprehensively, provided the errors are corrected by not considering partial words or by having the AI system learn to recognize and exclude such errors through recursive processes. The initial input prompt was insufficient; therefore, it is necessary to provide it and verify that it has been understood and applied. This verification must be requested every time ChatGPT generates the spreadsheet on which the data reading will be based.

Further considerations aligned with these findings stem from additional elements transversally impacting various research phases and substantiating the researchers' sense of uncertainty during the activity. If researchers cannot resume where previous dialogue sessions with ChatGPT left off, they must re-upload research materials after each interruption. Despite this, ChatGPT demonstrated inconsistent operation, identifying a total number of texts different from 173 (e.g., 71, 174), even with the same file and identical prompts. Regarding research value, this inconsistency required constant oversight by the researcher, who had to instruct ChatGPT multiple times to ensure it read all 173 texts of the corpus, and these activities yielded inconsistent results. The timing of the activities significantly affects the results; the confidence a researcher might have in resuming analysis later, relying on precise annotations of each step (completed and to be completed), must be reconsidered when using ChatGPT. The relationship with the tool must be redefined, likely in light of ChatGPT's update peculiarities, which configure different scenarios depending on the ongoing updates.

An extensive research and reflection area remains open to evaluate the possibility of using ChatGPT in content analysis, particularly in qualitative methodology where the AI's ability to simulate human thought (Kaplan J., 2018) could add value to the analysis, an aspect that remains to be fully experienced.

Further reflections can be conducted on AI functionalities that can be integrated into content analysis software, activated intentionally, potentially leading to more insights, particularly for the qualitative dimension of text research.

Analyzing AI-created content offers a unique insight into how these technologies can be used to understand and improve the creative process. Additionally, it has significant potential in pathways dealing with self-awareness and self-efficacy.

References

Batini F., *Del Sarto G. Narrazioni di narrazioni.* Orientamento narrativo e progetto di vita. Trento. Erickson; 2005.

Bruner, J. S. *La fabbrica delle storie. Diritto, letteratura, vita* (Making stories: law, literature, life). Milano. Laterza; 2020.

Bruner, J. S. *La mente a più dimensioni* (In search of mind: Essays in autobiography). Milano. Laterza; 2013.

Bruner, J. S. *La ricerca del significato.* Per una psicologia culturale (Acts of meaning: four lectures on mind and culture). Milano. Bollati Boringhieri; 1992.

Foucault, M. *Tecnologie del sé* (Technologies of the self: A Seminar with Michel Foucault). Milano. Bollati Boringhieri; 1992.

Kaplan J. *Intelligenza artificiale. Guida al prossimo futuro* (Artificial Intelligence: what everyone needs to know®). Milano. LUISS University Press; 2017.

Messuri I., Balleri L. *Narrarsi attraverso: il nome proprio in autobiografia.* Studi sulla Formazione: 27, 181-1, 2024-1, doi: 10.36253/ssf-15156.

Reiter, E. & Dale, R. Building Applied Natural Language Generation Systems. Cambridge University Press, 1997 https://web.science.mq.edu.au/~rdale/publications/papers/1997/jnle97.pdf.

Chapter 9

The Impact of Artificial Intelligence on Creative Teaching: An Investigation of Education in the Technological Age

Sabrina Lucilla Barone[*]
Pegaso Telematic University, Naples, Italy

Abstract

The evolution of education in the artificial intelligence (AI) era raises critical questions about transforming educational processes (Papert, 1993). The growing interaction between various technologies and creativity offers new perspectives and challenges for contemporary teaching. The integration of AI as a mediator in teaching and learning processes has the potential to revolutionise educational methodologies (Koedinger & Corbett, 2006; UNESCO, 2019a). This approach may foster a future of personalised, inclusive learning environments (Coppi, 2018; Di Palma, 2023), placing the learner at the centre and catering to individual needs. However, issues regarding safeguarding originality in creative expression and promoting autonomous critical thinking are also emerging. Teachers are crucial in guiding students through the responsible use of technology, stimulating creativity (Csikszentmihalyi, 1996; Luckin, 2017, 2018), and providing a mindful learning environment. Critical reflection on AI's ethical, social, and pedagogical implications in education is essential to ensure the equitable and ethical use of the technology. Through an analysis of student opinions and questionnaires, it is possible to evaluate student perceptions of AI, their

---

[*] Corresponding Author's Email: sabrinalucilla.barone@unipegaso.it

In: Computational Arts and Creative Products
Editor: Alessandra Micalizzi
ISBN: 979-8-89530-426-6
© 2025 Nova Science Publishers, Inc.

awareness of its risks, and the impact of AI on the educational experience. This study explored the dynamic link between creativity and AI in education, recognising the centrality of creative and critical development as a priority objective of contemporary education (Robinson, 2001).

Keywords: creativity, technologies, education

The New Era of AI

Artificial intelligence (AI) is a true revolution due to its transformative impact on various sectors, including education. This multifaceted and ever-evolving field, characterised by diverse definitions, can be broadly understood as the ability of artificial systems to mimic human intelligence through learning, reasoning, and autonomous action (Russell & Norvig, 2020). AI systems can learn from data and experience, improving their performance through machine learning, deep learning, and positive reinforcement (Goodfellow et. al., 2016). They can reason about information and make logical decisions, analyse data, identify patterns and draw conclusions, and act in the real world without direct human intervention; for instance, AI can perform tasks such as autonomous driving, translating languages, and writing creative texts (Nilsson, 1998).

There are different types of AI, each with specific characteristics and applications. Narrow AI focuses on a specific task or domain, such as facial recognition or playing chess. Artificial general intelligence (AGI) is a theoretical form of AI that would possess intelligence equivalent to or superior to that of humans in various fields, and artificial superintelligence (ASI) is a stronger hypothetical form of AI that would surpass human intelligence and capabilities in all aspects (Chollet, 2018).

A Long Evolutionary Path

The evolutionary path of AI has deep roots in the mathematical and computer science theories and advances of the 20th century. One of the first significant moments in AI was Alan Turing's proposal of the Turing test in 1950, a fundamental idea that still challenges the scientific community today (Turing, 1950). In the 1950s and 1960s, pioneers such as Marvin Minsky and John McCarthy helped to define the first algorithmic approaches to AI, developing fundamental concepts such as neural networks and symbolic logic (McCarthy, 1959; Minsky, 1967). Although the 1970s and 1980s saw a phase of stagnation known as the 'AI winter', progress resumed in the 1990s with the development of machine learning, leading to a resurgence of connectionism, a paradigm inspired by the functioning of the human brain (Hopfield, 1982; Rumelhart et al., 1986). In the new millennium, increasingly complex algorithms and an abundance of data have led to the emergence of practical applications across a wide range of industries, with world-renowned platforms investing heavily in AI to improve their services and products (Mitchell, 1997).

AI now has a significant impact in many fields, such as medicine, finance, music, transportation, and manufacturing, with applications that continue to grow and evolve, radically transforming how we live and work (Boden, 2019).

AI and Education

Italian education has experienced an unprecedented evolution, characterised by significant legislative and pedagogical transformations over the centuries. Starting from the legislative foundations of the 19th century (Romano, 2005), the education system is today characterised by the adoption of new technologies and AI. Because it created the need for distance learning, the COVID-19 pandemic has played a decisive role in accelerating this transformation (Tam & El-Azar, 2020). Schools have adopted e-learning platforms and digital tools, enabling students to participate in virtual lessons and to access online resources from anywhere and at any time (Gennari et al., 2023). Following the resolution of the pandemic crisis, technology emerged as a critical tool in fostering a positive classroom climate, enhancing student motivation, and improving student focus.

AI is radically transforming the world of education by disrupting the traditional teaching and learning paradigm. One of the main innovations introduced by AI is personalisation: machine learning algorithms analyse student data to create unique learning paths, tailoring content and teaching methods to individual needs and preferences (Luckin et al., 2016). This approach increases learning effectiveness and student engagement, making education more engaging and targeted to actual needs.

Furthermore, AI has enabled the automation of administrative and assessment tasks, freeing up teachers' time teachers and allowing them to focus on more creative and interactive aspects of their work. For example, automated grading systems can mark assignments and tests, providing immediate feedback to students and identifying areas that need further reinforcement (Williamson, 2017).

Another surprising innovation is virtual tutors, who assist students in real-time, answering their questions and guiding them through complex learning materials. These AI-based tutors can provide continuous support, regardless of the time of day or length of lessons, ensuring more flexible and accessible learning (Anderson et al., 1995).

AI also facilitates predictive analytics by using large amounts of data to identify students at risk of dropping out or failing early, allowing for timely and targeted interventions (Siemens & Long, 2011). Furthermore, integrating augmented and virtual reality technologies, enhanced by AI, creates immersive learning environments that can improve the understanding of complex concepts and stimulate creativity (Csikszentmihalyi, 1996; Luckin, 2017, 2018).

Despite these advances and because the phenomenon of 'datafication' also concerns the education sector, it is crucial to address the ethical implications of AI at the social level and in education to ensure the protection of student data (Mayer-Schönberger & Cukier, 2013). Promoting equity in access to technologies and preserving originality and the primacy of creative capacity are vital goals. Furthermore, AI should not replace the role of teachers but rather enhance it, strengthening their role as facilitators and mediators of learning.

The problems related to students' use of technology have long been at the centre of reflection and discussion in the scientific community.

Given the increasing pervasiveness of AI across all knowledge domains, including education, and its seemingly unstoppable progress driving potentially unpredictable innovations, a crucial concern emerges: As primary users of these technologies, students might lack sufficient awareness of the potential risks associated with AI use, particularly regarding its impact on their creativity and originality.

We are witnessing widespread educational poverty, the result of a weakening of critical thinking specifically, the overabundance of stimuli from the Internet, especially social media, hinders the development of reflective, critical, and creative thinking.

This undermines the ability to analyse represented events and to elaborate a personal construction of meaning (Carr, 2011).

Consequently, a reasonable hypothesis is that the massive introduction of AI in education may negatively influence students' creativity and that they are not entirely aware of the risks and consequences of inappropriate use.

Many questions arise from these considerations, among which are the following:

What are students' opinions about AI? Do they believe it can implement, support, and improve the learning experience regarding inclusiveness?

Do they consider AI a new technology that, combined with human creativity, opens up new scenarios heralding expressive and cultural potential, or, on the contrary, do they consider it a threat to creative freedom?

What role do they attribute to the teacher's function?

It is on these questions that the present investigation focused on.

Research Study

Focusing on participants: Ten classes from Regina Margherita State High School in Salerno, Italy, participated in a study designed to address the research questions, namely five classes of section A (Human Sciences branch) and five of section L (Linguistics branch) from the first to the fifth, involving a total of 224 students (including 12 Bes students).

The study focused on a single specific case and endeavoured to highlight the transferability of the results rather than make statistical generalisations. Case studies aim at specific objectives by combining qualitative and quantitative data; however, they can be limited by subjectivity and the difficulty of generalisation, thus requiring considerable resources and time for in-depth analysis (Biancone & Cisi, 2017; Trinchero, No Year).

Section III: Answer the following questions, assigning a score from 1 to 5, where 1 corresponds to the minimum and 5 the maximum. Assign the other ratings of 2, 3, or 4 for all intermediate cases.	1	2	3	4	5
To what extent can introducing artificial intelligence (AI) in education improve students' learning experience?					
How much do you think AI can personalise education to suit your needs better than traditional teaching methods can?					
To what extent do you believe that AI can foster more creative and innovative learning, understood as a process that encourages the generation of original ideas, innovative solutions, and the exploration of new approaches, especially in educational contexts such as school training, university education, or vocational training?					
To what extent can teachers play a fundamental role in promoting student creativity?					

Figure 1. Example questions.

The instrument used was a questionnaire designed to evaluate students' opinions of, use of, and relationship with AI.

The questionnaire was divided into three sections: the first collected demographic information (age, gender, school address), the second assessed knowledge and use of AI, and the third was the actual questionnaire and was reserved exclusively for those who declared that they knew about and used AI to complete study activities. Figure 1 presents some of the questions in Section III.

Method and Times

In May 2024, we administered the questionnaire online via Google Forms during extracurricular hours.

Participants responded using a 5-point Likert scale.

No time limit was imposed. We protected participant anonymity by not recording names or email addresses.

Of the 224 students invited to participate, 186 responded voluntarily; in terms of demographics, they were variously distributed by school, age, and gender (Figure 2).

The first number indicates the age, the second the frequency, and the third the %.

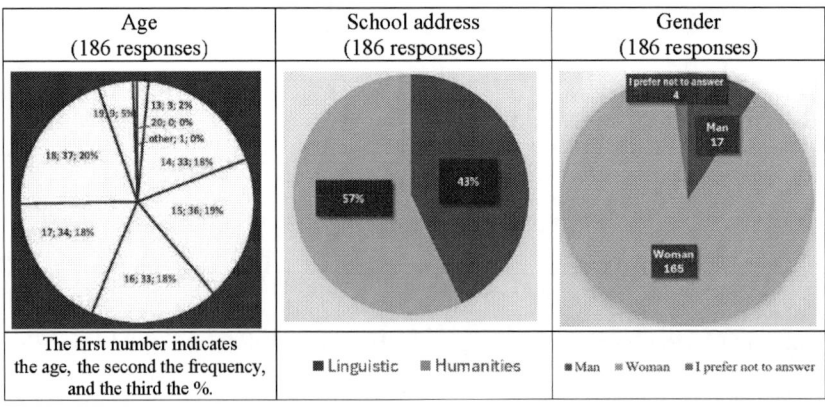

Figure 2. Demographics.

Of those interviewed, 95% declared that they knew of AI, and 58.9% said that they used it in normal study activities (summaries, research, translations, writing essays, etc.), even if their use was often marginal and not substantial. As a result, only 109 students had access to the third section of the questionnaire.

The responses revealed an optimistic perception regarding the potential of AI. Students recognise its role in improving the learning process by making it more engaging and in tune with their interests. In addition, they appreciate how AI facilitates access to learning materials, personalises learning, and can adapt to different individual needs and cognitive styles. This promotes inclusion and helps create a more equitable and accessible educational environment for all.

Students are optimistic about creativity, believing AI can encourage and support it, thus promoting innovation without compromising originality.

Furthermore, they do not consider human intelligence and AI to be in direct competition, as they consider AI creations incomparable to the genius of the human mind. Human intelligence is characterised by variety and dynamism, distinctive and unique elements incapable of replication by machines.

The answers reflect an overall positive opinion of AI, with students recognising its considerable potential but maintaining a cautious stance in regard to the limits and impacts of its interaction with the traditional learning process.

This study revealed the fundamental role of the teacher: technologies can be integrated both in the classroom and at home for in-depth analysis without replacing the presence and role of the teacher, who acts as an indispensable mediator in an active and ethical approach to learning and serves as a fundamental guide in the responsible use of this extraordinary resource. Students recognise that not all teachers have such advanced technological skills to use AI as a support tool for teaching activities and the transformation of educational processes (Papert, 1993).

Some Reflections

The students' opinions align with the most optimistic perspectives in the literature, as they highlight the benefits of AI in teaching and school training, overshadowing the risks (Carr, 2011; Ceruti, 2017; Di Donato, 2024). AI is a wave that we must learn to ride, dominate, and expertly manage in order not to be overwhelmed by it. One thing is sure: We cannot oppose progress or go back.

From the analysis of the answers provided by the students, some suggestions emerge which, at least in part, answer the initial questions:

- AI cannot compete with human intelligence in creativity and the production of original works for several fundamental reasons. Human creativity is closely linked to self-awareness, emotional experience, and reflective capacity. Human beings use their experiences and emotions to generate original ideas and unique works of art. In contrast, AI operates on preexisting algorithms and data, lacking consciousness and subjective experience (Boden, 1998). While AI can mimic human creativity, its works are derivative and lack true originality because they are limited by what has already been coded (McCormack et al., 2019). Human creativity breaks patterns, explores new directions in unpredictable and innovative ways, creates unexpected connections, and develops new concepts. Existing models limit AI, preventing true innovation.

Furthermore, producing unique works requires emotional involvement and an understanding of cultural nuances that AI cannot replicate. Human artists infuse their work with their personal vision and experiences, creating works that resonate universally (Colton, 2012). Human creativity thrives on curiosity and a yearning to discover the unknown, qualities that are absent in AI, which is programmed solely to optimise and replicate (Runco, 2004). Therefore, AI cannot compete with human intelligence in creativity and producing original (imperfect and therefore unique) works due to a lack of awareness, emotional experience, improvisational ability, authentic innovation, and deep cultural connection.

- The introduction of technologies and AI has brought significant innovations in teaching, but the role of the teacher remains central and irreplaceable. Teachers provide emotional support and human connection critical to student well-being, aspects that technologies cannot fully replicate (Brown et al., 2016). They can tailor lessons to individual needs, providing personalised and contextualised education (Darling-Hammond, 2006; Hattie & Timperley, 2007). Technology can automate repetitive tasks, allowing teachers to focus on more strategic and relevant teaching activities. Furthermore, teachers are essential in teaching social values, civil behaviours, and interpersonal skills, which are essential for forming responsible citizens (UNESCO, 2015). They also promote creativity and critical thinking in students (Robinson, 2006), essential skills for meeting real-world challenges. Finally, teachers act as mentors and role models, inspiring and guiding students' learning and personal growth (Fullan, 1993), providing emotional support, personalising learning, and developing social and civic competencies in their students (Johnson et al., 2017)—indispensable soft skills!

Ceruti asserted the following: 'Today's students acquire a great deal of information [...] in a fragmentary way, without any interpretative filter and any educational perspective capable of [...] making the multiple experiences and the overall educational path of each person coherent' (2017, p. 15). The teacher represents that interpretative filter capable of generating meaningful learning and promoting complex and multidimensional knowledge that is appropriate to address the complexity and multidimensionality of the knowledge objects and problems that characterise the new global human condition, including information obesity (Berloco, 2019).

Although technologies can improve the learning experience, the role of the teacher remains irreplaceable due to their ability to provide emotional support, personalise learning, and develop social and civic skills (Johnson et al., 2017). Soft skills are surely essential!

- AI in education can improve school inclusion by adapting content to individual abilities and providing targeted support to students with special needs (Luckin et al., 2016). Technologies such as speech recognition and translation applications increase accessibility for students with disabilities (Alper & Raharinirina, 2006). AI also allows for the early diagnosis of learning difficulties, facilitating timely interventions (Holmes et al., 2019); promotes access to education for marginalised groups, including refugees and nonattending students; and personalises learning through individualised study plans. Virtual teaching assistants support teachers by automating routine tasks and allowing them to dedicate more time to students. Finally, AI helps in correcting tests and essays (Mizumoto & Eguchi, 2023) and supports learning, especially in developing countries (Pedró et al., 2019).

- AI promotes digital literacy by preparing students for a future life and career strongly involving technology (Heffernan & Koedinger, 2012; Unesco, 2019b; Cormann, 2023). However, one problem is teachers who may not be up to date with technology; they may often not be experts in technology and sometimes may view them sceptically, fearing more risks than benefits. Recent surveys have revealed that only 11% of teachers have in-depth knowledge of AI, while 54% use it for teaching (Orizzontescuola.it, 2024). Ensuring ethical implementation thereof requires addressing challenges related to privacy and algorithmic bias (Williamson, 2017; Noble, 2018), and the role of the teacher as a mediator remains crucial. Closing the AI skills gap requires not only the adoption of advanced technologies but also a reconsideration of teaching content and methods at all levels of education.
- The ethical implications connected to the improper use of AI (of which students have no awareness) are of extreme importance and deserve careful reflection, especially in light of two emerging phenomena: first, the escape from the present towards virtual and parallel worlds disconnected from reality, and second, the ambition of some to transfer their consciousness to achieve a sort of immortality.

AI has made it possible to create incredibly realistic and immersive virtual environments. These parallel worlds offer people a refuge from reality, often full of problems and difficulties. However, this escape from the present can have negative consequences. There is a risk that people disconnect from reality, preferring to live in artificial worlds where they control every aspect of their experience. This can lead to significant social isolation, reducing individuals' ability to face real-life challenges and develop authentic relationships (Turkle, 2011; Schroeder, 2012). Furthermore, addiction to virtual worlds can contribute to mental health problems, such as depression and anxiety (Elhai et al., 2017).

Another critical ethical issue concerns the ambition of some to transfer their consciousness into digital forms to achieve immortality. This idea, although still theoretical, raises numerous ethical questions. First, there is the issue of identity: Can a digital copy of a person's consciousness be considered the same person (Kurzweil, 2005)? Furthermore, achieving digital immortality could create new forms of inequality, where only those who can afford such technologies can escape death (Bostrom, 2005). This could further exacerbate social and economic disparities. Finally, there is a risk that such technologies will be exploited in unethical ways, such as by government or corporate entities manipulating or controlling digital consciousnesses (Floridi, 2013).

These scenarios raise complex questions that require in-depth discussion and a robust regulatory framework. Careful consideration of the ethical implications of AI is essential for developing appropriate guidelines and regulations to ensure that these technologies are used to promote human well-being and social justice (Mittelstadt et al., 2016).

Conclusion

This survey investigated students' knowledge of, attitudes towards, and practical use of AI in education. Additionally, it aimed to identify opportunities and challenges associated with integrating AI into educational settings. The sample involved 10 classes from two different addresses of a high school in Salerno. It was essential for students to reflect on the intriguing topic of AI because it can both support and redefine educational practices and pose a potential risk for training processes.

This case study's limited scope, focusing on a few classes in a single school, necessitates further research in broader and more diverse contexts.

The most significant fact that emerged from the study is the interconnection between creativity and intelligence: the progress of one favours that of the other. The machine will never be able to replace man, who is endowed with emotional consciousness, feelings, and free will (Andler, 2024; Faggin, 2024). Consequently, it will never be able to replace the teacher, a precious guide on the journey of knowledge. Man dominates machines, and AI remains a tool that assists man. In fact, despite being able to simulate human intelligence and generate creative results, AI lacks the rigorous methodological approach that characterised, for example, the birth of modern science (Cartesio, 2014) and cannot replicate the human experience. AI systems, such as those based on machine learning and deep learning, operate on probability and principles of statistical correlation, breaking down complex problems into subproblems and solving them mathematically without understanding the meaning of the tasks or results. Though AI can optimise models through many iterations, these processes prioritise performance metrics over philosophically grounded control.

Toffler, who was not an opponent of progress but a pragmatist, argued that we need neither passive acceptance nor rigid opposition but a variety of creative strategies that allow us to selectively shape, direct, accelerate, or slow down change (Toffler, 1971).

The role of society and technology in the development of thinking is complex, and studies have not reached an unambiguous consensus, but there is one certainty: AI will continue to evolve and offer incredible new possibilities. It is, therefore, crucial to maintain a balanced perspective that values the irreplaceable role of the human being. We must start from man to return to man in a generative dimension (Mannese, 2023), with freedom not only as the cause of action but also as the horizon against which one acts with awareness and creativity. Future education must integrate AI as a support without losing sight of the value of creativity, emotions, and human intuition. Technologies must be at the service of man and not man at the service of technologies. Only in this way can we ensure harmonious and sustainable progress, where technology and humanity complement each other.

References

Alper, S., & Raharinirina, S. (2006). Assistive technology for individuals with disabilities: A review and synthesis of the literature. *Journal of Special Education Technology, 21*(2), 47-64.

Anderson, J. R., Corbett, A. T., Koedinger, K. R., & Pelletier, R. (1995). Cognitive tutors: Lessons learned. *The Journal of the Learning Sciences, 4*(2), 167-207.

Andler, D. (2024). *Il duplice enigma. Intelligenza artificiale e intelligenza umana (The dual enigma. Artificial intelligence and human intelligence).* Torino: Einaudi.

Berloco, R. (2019). I social network e il sovraccarico di informazioni (Social networks and information overload). Culturedigitali.org. https://www.culturedigitali.org/i-social-network-e-il-sovraccarico-di-informazioni/ (last access 08/07/2024).

Biancone, P. P., & Cisi, M. (2017). *Scoprire l'azienda. Casi di management (Discovering the company. Management cases).* Torino: Giappichelli.

Boden, M. A. (1998). Creativity and artificial intelligence. *Artificial Intelligence, 103*(1-2), 347-3.

Boden, M. A. (2019). *L'intelligenza artificiale: una guida per i curiosi (Artificial intelligence: a guide for the curious).* Bologna: Il Mulino.

Bostrom, N. (2005). Transhumanist values. *Review of Contemporary Philosophy, 4*, 3-14.

Brown, C. P., Schlomer, G. L., Fosco, G. M., & Manning, N. (2016). Understanding the role of supportive adults in young adolescents' lives: Implications for measurement and intervention. *Journal of Applied Developmental Psychology, 46*, 39-52.

Carr, N. (2011). *The shallows: What the internet is doing to our brains.* New York: W. W. Norton & Company.

Cartesio, R. (2014). *Discorso sul metodo (Method talk).* Santarcangelo di Romagna: Rusconi.

Ceruti, M. (2017). La scuola e le sfide della complessità (Schools and the challenges of complexity). *Studi Sulla Formazione/Open Journal of Education, 20*(2), 9-20. https://doi.org/10.13128/Studi_Formaz-22165 (last access 20 July 2024).

Chollet, F. (2018). *Deep learning with Python*. NY: Manning Publications.

Colton, S. (2012). The painting fool: Stories from building an automated painter. In *Computational creativity research: Towards creative machines* (pp. 3-38). Berlino: Springer.

Coppi, A. (2018). Arte e Oltre: Percorsi educativi multidisciplinari ed interculturali per l'inclusione a scuola (Art and Beyond: Multidisciplinary and intercultural educational paths for inclusion at school). *L'integrazione scolastica e sociale, 17*(2), 153-171.

Cormann, M. (2023). Il mondo del lavoro richiede nuove abilità per navigare con successo nell'era digitale e ambientale (The world of work requires new skills to successfully navigate the digital and environmental age). *Agenda Digitale*. https://www.agendadigitale.eu/ (last access 23 June 2024).

Csikszentmihalyi, M. (1996). *Creativity: Flow and the psychology of discovery and invention*. New York: HarperCollins.

Darling-Hammond, L. (2006). Constructing 21st-century teacher education. *Journal of Teacher Education, 57*(3), 300-314.

Di Donato, D. (2024). Tutti i rischi dell'uso precoce di smartphone e AI: gli studi (All the risks of early smartphone and AI use: studies). *Agenda Digitale.edu*. (last access 27 May 2024).

Di Palma, G. (2023). The role of artificial intelligence in personalized learning environments: A systematic review. *Journal of Educational Technology & Society, 26*(1), 65-78.

Elhai, J. D., Dvorak, R. D., Levine, J. C., & Hall, B. J. (2017). Problematic smartphone use: A conceptual overview and systematic review of relations with anxiety and depression psychopathology. *Journal of Affective Disorders, 207*, 251-259.

Faggin, F. (2024). Nessuna IA potrà mai sostituire l'uomo (No AI will ever replace man). *Ansa.it*. (last access 08/05/2024).

Floridi, L. (2013). *The ethics of information*. Oxford: Oxford University Press.

Fullan, M. (1993). *Change forces: Probing the depths of educational reform*. London: Routledge.

Gennari, R., Matera, M., Morra, D., Melonio, A., & Rizvi, M. (2023). Design for social digital well-being with young generations: Engage them and make them reflect. *International Journal of Human – Computer Studies, 173*, 103006.

Goodfellow, I., Bengio, Y., & Courville, A. (2016). *Deep learning*. Cambridge: MIT Press.

Hattie, J., & Timperley, H. (2007). The power of feedback. *Review of Educational Research, 77*(1), 81-112.

Heffernan, N. T., & Koedinger, K. R. (2012). Integrating assessment within educational technologies to improve learning: Creating adaptive learning technologies that are flexible and widely used. *International Journal of Artificial Intelligence in Education, 22*(2), 153-167.

Holmes, W., Bialik, M., & Fadel, C. (2019). *Artificial intelligence in education: Promises and implications for teaching and learning*. Center for Curriculum Redesign.

Hopfield, J. J. (1982). Neural networks and physical systems with emergent collective computational abilities. *Proceedings of the National Academy of Sciences, 79*, 2554-2558.
Johnson, D. W., Johnson, R. T., & Smith, K. A. (2017). Cooperative learning: Improving university instruction by basing practice on validated theory. *Journal on Excellence in College Teaching, 28*(2), 3-29.
Koedinger, K. R., & Corbett, A. T. (2006). Cognitive tutors: Technology bringing learning sciences to the classroom. In K. Sawyer (Ed.), *The Cambridge handbook of the learning sciences* (pp. 61-78). Cambridge: Cambridge University Press.
Kurzweil, R. (2005). *The singularity is near: When humans transcend biology.* New York: Viking.
Luckin, R. (2017). *Intelligence unleashed: An argument for AI in education.* London: Pearson Education Limited.
Luckin, R. (2018). *Enhancing learning and teaching with technology: What the research says.* London: UCL Institute of Education Press.
Luckin, R., Holmes, W., Griffiths, M., & Forcier, L. B. (2016). *Intelligence unleashed: An argument for AI in education.* London: Pearson.
Mannese, E. (2023). *Manuale di Pedagogia Generativa e Sistema-Mondo. Epistemologie e Comunità Pensanti per l'Homo Generativus (Handbook of Generative Pedagogy and World-System. Epistemologies and Thinking Communities for Homo Generativus).* Brescia: Pensa Multimedia.
Mayer-Schönberger, V., & Cukier, K. (2013). *Big Data: A Revolution That Will Transform How We Live, Work, and Think.* Londra: John Murray Publishers Ltd.
McCarthy, J. (1959). Programs with common sense. In *Teddington Conference on the Mechanization of Thought Processes* (pp. 75–91). London: Her Majesty's Stationery Office.
McCormack, J., Gifford, T., & Hutchings, P. (2019). Autonomy, authenticity, authorship and intention in computer-generated art. In *Proceedings of the Ninth International Conference on Computational Creativity* (pp. 196-203).
Minsky, M. (1967). *Computation: Finite and Infinite Machines.* Upper Saddle River, NJ: Prentice-Hall.
Mitchell, T. M. (1997). *Machine Learning.* New York: McGraw-Hill.
Mittelstadt, B. D., Allo, P., Taddeo, M., Wachter, S., & Floridi, L. (2016). The ethics of algorithms: Mapping the debate. *Big Data & Society, 3*(2), 2053951716679679.
Mizumoto, A., & Eguchi, M. (2023). Exploring the potential of using an AI language model for automated essay scoring. *Research Methods in Applied Linguistics, 2*, 100050.
Murphy, K. P. (2012). *Machine Learning: A Probabilistic Perspective.* Cambridge, MA: MIT Press.
Nilsson, N. J. (1998). *Artificial intelligence: A new synthesis.* Burlington, MA: Morgan Kaufmann.
Noble, S. U. (2018). *Algorithms of oppression: How search engines reinforce racism.* New York: University Press.
Orizzontescuola.it (2024). *"L'IA può essere una risorsa, ma la scuola deve aggiornarsi", l'appello della Gilda degli Insegnanti ("AI can be a resource, but the school must update itself", the appeal of the Gilda degli Insegnanti).* https://www.orizzontescuola.

it/lia-puo-essere-una-risorsa-ma-la-scuola-deve-aggiornarsi-lappello-della-gilda-degli-insegnanti/ (last access 27 May 2024).

Papert, S. (1993). *The Children's Machine: Rethinking School in the Age of the Computer.* New York: Basic Books.

Pedró, F., Subosa, M., Rivas, A., & Valverde, P. (2019). *Artificial intelligence in education: challenges and opportunities for sustainable development.* https://unesdoc.unesco.org/ark:/48223/pf0000366994 (last access 27 May 2024).

Robinson, K. (2001). Out of Our Minds: Learning to Be Creative. Bloomington, IN: Capstone.

Robinson, K. (2006). Do schools kill creativity? T*ED Talks.* https://www.ted.com/talks/ken_robinson_do_schools_kill_creativity (last access 26 May 2024).

Romano, M. (2005). *Storia dell'istruzione in Italia (History of education in Italy).* Roma: Laterza.

Rumelhart, D. E., Hinton, G. E., & Williams, R. J. (1986). Learning representations by back-propagating errors. *Nature, 323*(6088), 533-536.

Runco, M. A. (2004). Creativity. *Annual Review of Psychology, 55*, 657-687.

Russell, S., & Norvig, P. (2020). *Artificial Intelligence: A Modern Approach.* London: Pearson.

Schroeder, R. (ed.) (2012). *The social life of avatars: Presence and interaction in shared virtual environments.* Berlin: Springer Science & Business Media.

Siemens, G., & Long, P. (2011). Penetrating the Fog: Analytics in Learning and Education. *EDUCAUSE Review, 46*(5), 30-32.

Tam, G., & El-Azar, D. (2020). 3 ways the coronavirus pandemic could reshape education. *World Economic Forum,* retrieved from: https://www.weforum.org/agenda/2020/03/3-ways-coronavirus-is-reshaping-education-and-what-changes-might-be-here-tostay/ (last access 20 May 2024).

Toffler, A. (1971). *Lo shock del futuro (The shock of the future).* Milano: Rizzoli.

Trinchero, R. (No Year). *Lo studio di caso (The case study).* https://pedagogiasperimentaleonlinedfe.wordpress.com/lo-studio-di-caso/ (last access 03 May 2024).

Turing, A. M. (1950). Computing machinery and intelligence. *Mind, 59*(236), 433-460.

Turkle, S. (2011). Alone together: Why we expect more from technology and less from each other. New York: Basic Books.

UNESCO. (2015). *Rethinking education: Towards a global common good?* UNESCO Publishing.

UNESCO. (2019a). Istruzione 2030: Dichiarazione di Monaco (Education 2030: Munich Declaration). UNESCO. https://unesdoc.unesco.org/ark:/48223/pf0000377433 (last access 12 June 2024).

UNESCO. (2019b). A*rtificial Intelligence in Education: Challenges and Opportunities for Sustainable Development.* United Nations Educational, Scientific and Cultural Organization. https://unesdoc.unesco.org/ark:/48223/pf0000366994 (last access 30/04/2024).

Williamson, B. (2017). *Big Data in Education: The Digital Future of Learning, Policy and Practice.* Thousand Oaks: Sage.

About the Editor

Alessandra Micalizzi is an associate professor at Pegaso University and senior lecturer at the SAE Institute of Milan. She is a member of the Scientific Committee of the Research and Development Department. Moreover, she serves as the coordinator for the international master's degree in media practices. She also coordinates the Centre for Research in Digital Humanities at Pegaso University where she is leading an extensive project on the role of AI in creative production.

She graduated from IULM University with a degree in public relations and wrote an experimental thesis on online love and the impact of new technologies on emotional sharing. After completing her PhD in communication and new technologies, she earned a degree in psychology from the Catholic University of the Sacred Heart of Milan, which included a major project on happiness and positive technologies.

Micalizzi holds master's degrees in counselling with a psychodynamic approach (SISPI, Italy) and digital marketing (SUPSI, Switzerland).

She has collaborated with several academies and universities such as IULM University, IUSVe, IUSTo, the University of Padua, and the University of Milan. Notably, she was a postdoctoral fellow at IULM University for 4 years and lecturer at IED for over 6 years, teaching in the communication and design programs at the bachelor's level.

Currently Micalizzi is visiting lecturer at IUAV University (Venice) for the Master of Science in neuroscience applied to architectural design (NAaD) and at the University of Padua in the Master of Arts in social media and politics communication program. She is coordinator of the PhD in digital humanities at Pegaso University and vice president of Play-Ability.

She has led a CEI initiative project and served as the principal investigator for two national projects cofunded by PRIN and PNRR. These research opportunities allowed her to focus on two main topics: the applied use of games and music-production practices in metaverse environments.

Micalizzi is a member of the Italian Sociology Association (AIS) and the European Sociology Association (ESA). Additionally, she is editor for the international review journal *Narrare i Gruppi* as well as for *Humanities and Social Science Communication*. She also coordinates the open-access book series Communication Process and Cultural Practices for WriteUp.

Over the years, her research has centred on new media and communication processes. Her recent research interests include social practices in digital contexts, user interactions with new technological environments, and the application of a gender perspective to cultural industries.

Recently, Micalizzi has focused on creative media and cultural production, particularly the use of AI, while maintaining her interest in video games as new social contexts and spaces for education and formative practices.

Contributors

Foreword

Francesco D'Isa trained as a philosopher and digital artist, has exhibited his works internationally in galleries and contemporary art centres. He debuted with the graphic novel *I.* (2011) and has since published essays and novels with renowned publishers such as Hoepli, effequ, Tunué, and Newton Compton. His notable works include the novel *La Stanza di Therese* (2017) and the philosophical essay *L'assurda Evidenza* (2022). Most recently, he released the graphic novel *Sunyata* with Eris Edizioni in 2023, the first comic published in Italy created with AI, and the essay *La Rivoluzione Algoritmica Delle Immagini* for Sossella Editore (2024). Francesco serves as the editorial director for the cultural magazine *L'Indiscreto* and contributes writings and illustrations to various magazines, both in Italy and abroad. He is a professor of philosophy at the Lorenzo de' Medici Institute (Firenze) and of illustration and contemporary plastic techniques (AI) at LABA (Brescia).

Chapter Authors

Lara Balleri is a PhD student in digital humanities at Pegaso University. A sociopedagogical educator and andragogist, she is a member of several research groups, and she is a teaching tutor at IUL University in general and social pedagogy. Since 2009, she has worked in the education of adults and young people, focusing on guidance and skills development. Her main research interest is authobiographical narratives.

Sabrina Lucilla Barone is a PhD student in equity, diversity, and inclusion (XXXIX cycle) at Pegaso University. A permanent secondary-school teacher of literary subjects, she specializes in pedagogy, inclusion, and school well-being. She has published articles in scientific journals, including A-range journals, on equity and inclusive educational practices.

Alessandro Camatta, a sound engineer and producer, is currently pursuing a degree at the SAE Institute. Meticulous, creative, and deeply passionate about audio, he has released several tracks on streaming platforms in collaboration with emerging artists.

Giusy Caruso is chairwoman of the CREATIE Research Group at Royal Conservatoire Antwerp; promotor; artist-researcher; and professional concert pianist oriented towards the futuristic nexus of art, science, and technology. Her research explores new forms of human-machine interaction, such as the role of gestural technology (e.g., EMG and motion tracking) in creating XR performances, the analysis of gestures, and AI musicking via machine learning. She also studies human-to-human entrainment in cocreative projects that combine music, dance, theatre, and active audience participation.

Francesco Epifani, MBA, is a mathematician, economist, and PhD student in digital humanities at Pegaso University where his research project centres on medical humanities. As a healthcare manager, he has served as chief executive officer and chief strategy officer of public and private Italian and multinational companies. He is also an expert in healthcare economics and organization and teaches mathematical analysis, mathematics for applications, healthcare economics and organization, and corporate finance and strategy courses for master's degree programs in specialization schools in Italian and foreign universities. He has authored over 50 publications in high-impact journals and is part of internationally recognized research groups.

Luca Ferliga, an audio-production student at the SAE Institute in Milan, is a music producer, sound designer, and guitarist. In these roles, he combines his passion for music with his artistic talent as a painter. With a blend of technical skill and creativity, he explores new horizons in both audio and visual arts.

Fabrizio Festa has a degree in philosophy and is a composer, conductor, and researcher in the field of musical informatics, with a particular focus on sound topology and computational sonology. He is also a full professor at the Conservatory E. R. Duni in Matera and a member of several music associations, including the Italian Association of Music Informatics and Atena Musica.

Clémence Martel, soprano and performer, holds degrees in flute and classical singing from the conservatories of Paris, Rotterdam, and Lausanne. She specializes in contemporary music at the Neue Musik Studio of HMDK Stuttgart and has won the 2020 Prix de la Ville de Fribourg for contemporary music. She collaborated with the Haus der Geschichte in Stuttgart. Since 2022, she has been a member of the Cantiere Zero collective (Vienna) and has worked with the Divertimento Ensemble (Milan). As a transdisciplinary artist, she is involved in research-creation projects with institutions such as the École des Beaux-Arts de Paris and Ensea.

Fabio Morotti is a PhD student in IULM University's doctoral programme of visual and media studies. His academic and professional background focuses on a multidisciplinary approach and is based on using anthropological categories for the analysis and understanding of contemporary visual culture. His research interests deal with AI-generated cinema, intangible heritage, Cambodian performing arts, aerial cinematography, and travel literature.

Elisa Poli is the research program leader at the Nuova Accademia di Belle Arti (NABA). From 2014 to 2021, she was responsible for the master's degree program in urban vision and architectural design at Domus Academy. She completed a PhD in architectural history from Université Paris 1 Panthéon-Sorbonne and cofounded the Cluster Theory Research Group. He has contributed to several architectural books and magazines, including *Domus*, *Icon Design*, *Abitare*, *Arch'it*, *AND*, *Paesaggio Urbano*, and *Archphoto*. Since 2010, he has been lecturing at conferences and Italian and international universities and institutions such as Middle East Technical University (METU) in Ankara, UA Faculty of Architecture in Antwerp, and the March Architecture School.

Alessandro Ratoci, composer, electronic performer and sound designer, holds degrees in musical composition, electronic music, and multimedia from the conservatory of Bologna, the HEM of Geneva, and IRCAM in Paris. Winner of the 2022 Franco Evangelisti prize, he focuses on research and practice of mixed music for computer and live human performers. Currently, he is a professor of electroacoustic composition at the conservatory Lucio Campiani in Mantua, Italy.

Mario Spada holds a degree in electronic music from the E. R. Duni Conservatory of Music and a second degree in pedagogical sciences. His work explores the interaction between AI and human creativity in the arts as well as virtual and augmented reality. He has participated in national and international projects and focuses on creating hybrid art forms.

Index

#

3D modelling, 29, 31

A

Ableton Live, 25, 29, 42, 74, 82
AI tool Chord Progression in FL Studio 24 (Beta), 70
AI-generated, vii, x, 5, 6, 7, 8, 29, 31, 42, 54, 80, 81, 105, 107, 120, 157
AI-generated cinema, 105, 107, 120, 157
AIneid, 105, 106, 110, 119
AIVA, vi, 25, 29, 42, 43, 68, 82
ambient music, 59, 68, 74
applied arts, ix, xi, 1
artificial creativity, v, 1, 5, 7, 10, 47, 48, 53, 54, 63, 64, 65, 84
artificial intelligence (AI), vi, vii, viii, ix, x, 1, 4, 5, 6, 7, 8, 9, 10, 11, 12, 13, 14, 18, 19, 20, 21, 22, 23, 25, 26, 29, 31, 41, 42, 43, 45, 47, 48, 49, 51, 54, 55, 58, 64, 65, 67, 68, 69, 70, 71, 72, 73, 75, 76, 77, 78, 79, 80, 81, 82, 83, 86, 89, 91, 93, 100, 105, 106, 107, 110, 116, 117, 118, 119, 120, 121, 122, 123, 125, 126, 127, 129, 130, 131, 134, 135, 137, 138, 139, 140, 141, 142, 143, 144, 145, 146, 147, 148, 149, 150, 151, 153, 154, 155, 156, 157, 158
artistic research, 13, 15, 22, 56
augmented reality (AR), 14, 16, 18, 26, 91, 92, 158
autobiography, vii, 125, 126, 135
avatars, 17, 18, 22, 151

B

baroque, 48, 50
Black Mirror, 83, 91, 103

C

capture technology (MoCap), 15, 16, 20
ChatGPT, vi, 18, 25, 29, 30, 34, 35, 39, 99, 125, 126, 127, 129, 130, 131, 132, 133, 134
chord progression, 70, 72, 73, 75, 78
ComfyUI, 108, 109, 120
computational creativity, 1, 5, 10, 11, 149
computer aided (or assisted) composition (CAC), 47, 56
content analysis, 126, 127, 128, 129, 130, 131, 133, 134
creative adversarial networks (CANs), 4
creative practices, 1, 21, 84
creativity, v, vii, 1, 2, 3, 4, 5, 6, 7, 8, 9, 10, 11, 12, 14, 20, 21, 29, 47, 48, 53, 54, 55, 57, 63, 64, 65, 73, 75, 79, 80, 81, 84, 101, 122, 125, 126, 137, 138, 140, 141, 143, 144, 145, 147, 148, 149, 150, 151, 156, 158
cultural products, 1, 4
cyberpunk, 42, 95
cyborg bodies, 87, 92

D

DALL-E, vi, 18, 25, 29, 31, 35, 36
deep learning, 1, 18, 75, 86, 138, 147, 149
digital audio workstations (DAWs), 72, 73, 74

E

education, vii, xi, 19, 129, 137, 138, 139, 140, 141, 144, 145, 146, 147, 148, 149, 150, 151, 154, 155
embodied cognition, 13, 15
EMG signals, 18
Euridyce, 62

F

Fight Club, 91, 92, 103
figurative checker, 118
film adaptation, 105

G

generative adversarial networks (GANs), 4, 5
generative AI, vi, 1, 4, 10, 11, 13, 14, 19, 49, 65, 69, 76, 91, 106, 110, 120, 121
gestural interface (GI), 19
Google Magenta Studio 2.0, 70, 75, 78

H

human-machine collaboration, 47

I

I-Artist, vii, 67, 79
interactive intelligence, 26
interactive technology, 13, 14, 20, 21

L

liquid art, 8, 81

M

machine learning (ML), 6, 10, 18, 20, 47, 58, 63, 64, 75, 77, 82, 86, 109, 112, 122, 126, 138, 139, 147, 150, 156
MAXQDA 24, 125, 126, 130, 132, 134
Mentimeter, 29, 44
Metaverse, 17, 22, 92, 93, 153

MIDI, 48, 63, 70, 75, 78
Midjourney, 99, 105, 106, 108, 109, 112, 114, 115, 116, 117, 119, 121, 122, 123
Midjourney Aeneid, 105
mixed music, 47, 48, 50, 63, 157
mixed reality, 26
music, vii, 1, 5, 8, 10, 11, 13, 14, 15, 16, 17, 18, 19, 20, 21, 22, 23, 26, 29, 41, 42, 43, 44, 45, 47, 48, 49, 50, 53, 54, 55, 56, 57, 58, 59, 60, 61, 63, 64, 65, 68, 69, 70, 72, 73, 74, 75, 76, 77, 78, 79, 80, 82, 85, 99, 139, 153, 156, 157, 158
music performance practice, 13, 14, 15, 16, 20, 21, 22

N

neural realm, 62
neural space, 31, 39, 40, 42, 44, 58
newness, 4

O

OpenMusic, 56
oracular synthesis, 61
Orpheus, 47, 48, 49, 50, 51, 52, 53, 54, 58, 59, 60, 61, 62, 64, 65
Orpheus mythology, 47

P

physicality, 17, 93
pop art, 1
popular music, 49, 68, 69
posthumanism, 83, 84, 85, 86, 89, 96, 100, 101, 102, 103
power, 35, 44, 54, 55, 64, 68, 73, 75, 87, 88, 90, 94, 96, 149
predictive medium, 110
Pro-C, 2, 3
proper name, 126, 129, 131

R

realtime audio variational autoencoder (RAVE), 19, 61, 62, 63, 64

Runway Gen-2, 108, 109

S

SmartComp, 72, 76, 78
SmartEQ, 72, 76, 79
sociological, 27, 28
spatial computing, 92, 93
synthesis, vi, 19, 25, 26, 29, 43, 44, 45, 56, 58, 61, 64, 65, 67, 82, 110, 121, 148, 150

T

technologies, v, vi, vii, viii, ix, xi, 1, 3, 4, 5, 6, 8, 9, 10, 13, 14, 15, 17, 20, 28, 47, 48, 54, 80, 81, 89, 90, 91, 92, 99, 100, 125, 126, 135, 137, 138, 139, 140, 143, 144, 145, 146, 147, 148, 149, 153

technology-enhanced-mirror, 16
temporal continuity, 128, 132, 133
text-to-image, 31, 105, 106, 107, 120, 121, 122
text-to-video, 107, 119
thematic coherence, 126, 127, 128, 132, 133
Tibre transfer, 47
Transhumans, 92

V

virtual reality (VR), 14, 16, 18, 22, 23, 25, 26, 29, 31, 35, 92, 93, 140
visual art, 1, 5, 53, 54, 84, 156
visual storytelling, vii, 105, 106, 110, 119
VR optimisation, 29